THE ADMISSIONS GAME

Gay Snow

CONTENTS

NOTE FROM THE AUTHOR

Applying to Elite Universities and Colleges is a miserable experience for everyone. Why is it miserable? Because most applicants who boast outstanding grades, perfect to near perfect standardized test scores, and stellar Extra-Curricular Activities get rejected. No one is spared, or so I thought.

Fast forward to March 2019, when the largest College admissions scandal emerged, dubbed 'Operation Varsity Blues' by the Federal Bureau of Investigation ("FBI"). We learned that our fellow brethren, parents just like us, were awoken in the early morning hours by FBI agents at their homes, who were armed with guns and arrest warrants. What the fuck was going on? This blockbuster Federal indictment rocked not only The World, but #OURWORLD.

The FBI pulled these folks out of their homes, and alleged these parents sought to get their kids accepted to Elite Schools via bribing College and standard testing Officials to alter academic and athletic records and standardized test scores.

This scandal confirmed our worst fear: the application process to Elite Schools was rigged. We were all stunned and sickened as we learned the sordid details of the criminal indictment.

When news of this scandal was first reported, my book was being edited. Talk about timing. It was also eerily prophetic.

Parents should encourage their kids to fulfill their own destiny based on their abilities. Bribing a variety of people who work within the Elite admissions process to inflate test scores, grades, and/or create bogus athlete profiles to *guarantee* an acceptance is how parents betray their own kid's intellectual ability. Not to mention the real victims in this story, the Qualified applicants who were denied admission because the Varsity Blues parents bought first-year seats for their less Qualified kids.

This book is a handbook on how parents should not only serve as role models, but to advocate for their kid. It is a 'no brainer', that parents should not alter official records or bribe officials to buy a guaranteed acceptance to an Elite School.

One last word before we embark on our journey to get your kid accepted to an Elite School. This book was written purely out of love. True. Throughout the years, my friends have urged me to write this book, to share our collective parenting experiences, and that bumpy ride we took to get our kids accepted to an Elite School. My intent was to make this journey not only informative, but fun.

My fellow parents, when you read this book, you will quickly observe that I deviated from a traditional writing style. This was consciously done to not only ensure that my tips, fun facts and wise words will be duly noted by you all, but to add a little humor as well.

Lastly, when you read a hashtag # word, my point is to emphasize the importance of that word. My kids have chastised me for not using the hashtag properly (only at the end of statement), but I really don't care. I need to get my point across to everyone.

INTRODUCTION

EXTRAORDINARY KIDS GET
ACCEPTED TO ELITE COLLEGES

Achievement. Success. Notoriety. Intellectual Superiority. Wealth. For decades, the Elite U.S. Colleges and Universities ("Schools") have been considered throughout the world to be symbolic of the American Dream. Historically, these fabled bastions of upper-class academia have been representative of an "Elite-Members Only Club," restricted to the children of the rulers of Corporate America, Government, Foreign Dignitaries or Hollywood Actors. Talk about prophetic. This was written prior to the Varsity Blues Scandal.

The mythical aura of these institutions is perpetuated by the universally perceived 'invite only' status granted solely to the crème de la crème of society, with the remaining crumbs spread to a lucky few. We (yes, you and me) want what the *Elite* have. We believe that a degree from an Elite School will grant our kids entrée into the fabled world of the affluent.

As my fellow parents prepare to embark on the Elite application journey, it is time for you to take an oath. Repeat after me, "Yes! I want my son/daughter to attend an Elite School for the above reasons and will do everything within my power to get him/her legally, legitimately accepted! 1 Caveat: I will not go to Jail." Congratulations, you are now an official member of the Crazy Parents Club!

Fast forward to the present day. The marble façades of these Colleges have opened their doors to welcome a more diverse community that reflects our current global, socio-economic society. These modern-day academic powerhouses now revel in prioritizing inclusion to maintain a global presence...

And that presence allows them to cherry-pick the best and brightest high school seniors that are spread throughout the world.

The 21st century is driven by a fast-paced global economy, in which highly intelligent and accomplished high school seniors are practically jumping over each other to get that golden ticket—the holy grail of acceptances to an Elite U.S. University or College.

Egos will be bruised, tears shed, hearts broken, and dreams shattered, but the allure of seizing the American dream of unparalleled success is a collective vision that inspires millions of aspiring students and their parents to go to incredible lengths.

I am speaking to you, my fellow brethren, parents. That is right, Mommy and Daddy. This book is totally geared towards the hyped-up, "crazy," parents who push their kids to be the best they can humanly be at every single 'thing' they do. #LOL, because it is true.

The goal for *all* of us (and I am included in this monkey barrel of parents) is to fulfill *our fantasy* of our kids attending an Elite School. But, and of course there is a but here, your kid is applying to School. Not you. You have already been there, done that. It is not about you anymore. Please, you must let go.

The problem with our master plan to get our kids into Elite Schools, is that we cannot get our kids into these Schools. Talk about a dream becoming nightmare! It is frustrating. The School application process has become the ultimate competition of students, not to mention their parents, vying for acceptance letters. Do I hear the whispers of a new reality TV show?

In this pressure-cooker environment it is not enough just to be a big fish in a little pond... a big fish must jump out of the water in order to be seen and heard by the Dean of Undergraduate Admissions. The Dean is the music producer of this entire album. She composed the song, wrote the lyrics, and now she is casting all the musicians. When applying to Elite Schools, your kid must sing aloud to a one-person audience, and that one person is the Dean.

The key to success is knowing What the Dean of Undergraduate Admissions *Wants* in Applicants. Elite Schools are *vying* for highly intelligent, innovative candidates to 'rock' their world. The Dean is on the lookout for the next Steve Jobs, Elon Musk, Mark Zuckerberg, or the person who will find the cure for cancer.

In this era of technological advancement, the future is now. By virtue of the technology that pervades our daily lives, parents are more empowered than ever to help create opportunities for their kid to follow their #PASSION. These parents are forward thinkers and emphatically believe that a "traditional" approach to child-rearing does not cut it for today's kids. They look beyond the established boundaries in education that have acted as a pipeline to traditional career paths (think accountant, investment banker, etc.), and want their kids to strengthen critical thinking skills to apply to coding, creating, and developing cutting edge concepts on a global level.

THE DISRUPTOR

This generation is striving towards writing the next best-selling video game, coding the newest must-have app, and producing the next Grammy-winning rap album. Once in a blue moon, there comes along a person who acts as *The Disruptor*, that rare breed who comes in swinging and radically transforms some component of our daily life in a big way. Perhaps they will introduce a new tech platform or device that electrifies our society with irrational excitement. We wait for the Disruptor to come, as if they are the next Messiah.

#WISEWORDS: The Dean wants the Disruptor.

Today's tech advancements have been reshaping the workforce and creating new careers for years. Our kids' education system is just S-L-O-W-L-Y inching its way forward to meet the growing demands of the 21st century. So, it is up to us, as parents, to provide our children with the space and support to cultivate their #PASSION(S). Take a page out of my playbook. This is how parents *empower* their kids to be #INNOVATIVE.

It is the Extraordinary teenager that will not only find success in the 21st Century but has a good chance to receive the coveted acceptance to an Elite School. Why do you ask? I will tell you. These kids have been skillfully trained to think outside of the box and encouraged to go beyond the status quo.

#WISEWORDS: Your goal is to raise kids to be Extraordinary.

What makes me a self-proclaimed expert to dole out advice to desperate parents and kids who get sucked into the black hole of Elite Schools admissions? I am the mother of two sons and helped get them accepted to an Elite University despite having zero connects.

Yes, and my sons encouraged me to share with my fellow brethren, a few 'tricks of the trade' I picked up throughout the years to raise them to not only get accepted to an Elite School, but to be extraordinary and thrive in the 21st century. I encouraged them to forge their own path and not be that cookie cutter kid!

As you read this book, consider this as a roadmap of how to raise kids to reach their full intellectual, academic, and social potential, so they can realize their personal achievement in life and thrive in the 21st century work force.

Working to accomplish these goals is not easy. It takes years to accomplish. Often there will be tears, frustration, or the inevitable yelling match that breaks out between parents and Elite-Schools-applying-to-high-school-seniors, so we must try to find some humor in this process.

This book holds the secrets for moving obstacles, and sometimes even boulders, out of your kids' ways, so they can achieve anything...within reason and within the limits of the law.

Oy vey, good luck. You need it.

#MOTIVATED#STRONGMAMAS#POSITIVEENERGY

#BELIEVE

CHAPTER 1

HOW TO MAKE AN ORDINARY KID EXTRAORDINARY IN THE 21ST CENTURY!

We need to address my mantra to make *ordinary kids #EXTRAOR-DINARY*. First and foremost, this really sounds like a magic trick, trying to turn kids into something other than what they appear to be. Better yet, it looks like a nose up to the naysayers, mentoring your kid to exceed traditional expectations.

Raising children is no easy task. I took the title of mom very seriously, because I wanted my sons to be active participants not only in their community but in the world. I believe that people should aspire to be a part of solutions, not problems, and never take a passive role in society.

As a parent, I had extremely high expectations for my kids to succeed at everything they attempted. They were not expected to be perfect. They were expected to, at minimum, *try* their best. In my mom eyes, their best was always exceptional, because they applied themselves. It was a high standard, but it was the standard I believed to be *reasonable* for them.

#NEVERACCEPTLESS.

Academics were no exception to my rule. The expectation was to achieve excellence, which was simply defined as straight "A's" in all subjects, with grades between 95-100%. Now, I am confident you are thinking I was (or am) crazy because you believe it would have been unrealistic to expect my sons to perform at that high standard. Well guess what? I am not the only parent that expects their kids to achieve perfect grades.

For me, it was a very realistic expectation that my sons achieved excellence in academics, because I knew they *could.*

When you raise your kids to always strive towards achieving their personal best, the next logical step is to raise the bar again.

Over time, parents do not need to raise the bar, because their kid assumes responsibility over their own destiny.

I realize that it is hard enough to raise a child to be ordinary, let alone to be extraordinary. But, the most important reason not to be ordinary is that life is short. As human beings, we should always want to push beyond boundaries that are either within or out of our control.

Knowledge is power, and the more we challenge ourselves to achieve, the more we can enhance our lives and our community.

◆ ◆ ◆

HOLD UP (which means, wait a minute) ...

Why do you want to raise a kid to be extraordinary? I say, "Why not?" Most people just want their kids to say please, thank you, and make eye contact when talking. Ordinary can be boring, no spark, no PASSION. I define an extraordinary kid as creative, inventive, passionate. In this instant, extraordinary kids goes beyond boundaries, and this is exactly what the Dean wants in an applicant!

Please, do not gloss over my mantra. If you do not agree with it, that is fine; everyone is entitled to their own opinion. I believe that all parents and mentors play a pivotal role in the development of children. Who are the winners in all of this? Your kids.

The question I pose to parents is, "When do you start preparing your kids academically and emotionally for an Elite School, or, on a broader scope, to be innovators in life?"

This question provides the foundation for this book. Do you start getting your kid ready for Elite Schools at the start of high school or elementary school? For high achieving families, the answer is at birth. You all know this is no joke. There are some families that will expose their babies in utero to Mozart, to stimulate intellectual growth...but even I will not go that far. Well, I may have done it once or twice. Who remembers?

CHAPTER 2

THE ALL OR NOTHING ATTITUDE FOR
ELITE COLLEGES & UNIVERSITIES

I know why you are reading this book. You are 'that parent' whose sole purpose in life up until this very moment has been to do anything and everything for your kid. Your goal is to get your high school junior or senior into the College or University of *your* dreams. And this is not just any *School*...it is an 'Elite' School.

REMEMBER: Excuse me, but *You, my fellow parent,* are not applying to Elite Schools! Whatever that dream school may be, it should be *your kid's* dream, not yours.

Now I am compelled to share a few tid-bits about me, so you can understand why I have appointed myself the Amateur Guru on Getting Kids Accepted to the Best Schools in the Country. I, too, have personally endured countless years of self-inflicted pain and torture, all in the name of getting my sons into an Elite University.

After folding up my legal career and tucking it away with the mothballs, I committed to be the all-in mom. No, I am not a martyr, although you can detect a bit of that martyrdom tone. Perhaps, I was not intellectually stimulated as a mom and needed a project. Who knows...

What really did me in, was watching my friend drive her daughter *nuts* for several years to have a perfect GPA and SAT score in order to attend her Elite College alma mater. That hurled me over the edge to the crazy world of applying to Elite Schools. My life would never be the same. It is all 'her' fault and I will not reveal her identity. She knows who she is!

My sons wanted to attend an Elite School. It was their choice. As the mom, I did not want them to get lost in the Elite application maze. I made it my mission to learn how the Elite application process 'really' worked. It turns out I was pretty good at it. I became 'Mommy Mountain Mover'. Fellow friends and parents came to know me as the How-to-Push-Your-Kid Whisperer, Pull-the-Rabbit-out-of-a-Hat Mom. Simply stated, I never lost sight of the endgame, which was to get these kids #ACCEPTED.

Parents who are hell-bent on getting their kids accepted into an Elite School are understandably, desperate people. Yes desperate, as in we have that 'deer in headlights' look in our eye. That inescapable feeling of helplessness is due to our inability to control the admissions process.

For years, while our kids were attending grades K-12, we parents were drinking endless gallons of figurative Kool-Aid. It was served to us at all of the sporting events, school plays, concerts, and parent-teacher nights, and it tasted like the vision of getting our kids accepted to every Elite School imaginable.

We drank the Kool-Aid like the refreshing summer beverage it was and were quickly brainwashed into believing that if we had our kids participate in every single extra-curricular activity and master *everything* they did, we could ensure their receipt of a golden acceptance letter...Talk about crazy, not to mention unrealistic.

I have been a long-time card-carrying member of the Crazy Parents' Club. I, like many before me, believe that the quality and level of education experienced in the *unique* setting of Elite Schools will provide my kids the foundation for *profound* future success. I emphasize the word 'profound,' because parents who ascribe to this belief, maintain that if their kid does not get accepted to an Elite Institution, their post-Secondary School life with be devoid of financial success and privilege.

On a deeper level, too, these parents believe that an Elite School's rejection of their kid will mean that they, as parents, have somehow *failed*. Sounds to me a little harsh and sad for us parents to feel this way. But we do. Thank heaven for therapy!

Clearly, the Elite application process makes Parents feel *vulnerable*. Despite achieving their own professional success, and sometimes even being lucky enough to wield unimaginable power in their respective careers, all parents are rendered utterly helpless when their kid applies to Elite Schools.

It is out of their hands, and these parents must bow down to the Elite Admissions Office, the Dean. For some parents who are accustomed to ruling their lives, and (yes, I am about to say it) their kid's lives, that kind of deference is #HARDTOSWALLOW.

Excuse me? Do I detect a hint of disbelief? I dare you to watch parents attend a College admissions event. These parents are in panic mode! At first glance, they appear calm, cool as cucumbers, dressed in blazers and khakis. I say Ha! They are sitting on the edge of their seats, plotting how to catapult their kid into standing next to the Dean of Undergraduate Admissions for a #GOODIMPRESSION.

Just recounting this scenario makes me want to vomit. I have been in that room. I have stood in the line of parent-child duos as we waited to shake the Dean's hand and tried desperately to list every reason our kid was phenomenal in the one long breath that the handshake lasted.

We had no shame. Looking back now, I cannot help but laugh at the absurdity of thinking that our 2-minute interaction with the Dean would somehow leave the perfect lasting impression to jolt my kid's application into the admit pile.

The Elite admissions process can seem like a mad scramble at times. But there are real, legitimate steps you can take to focus your energies and efforts in a productive manner. So please, stop wasting your time on admission events. You have bigger fish to fry!

THE DIFFERENCE BETWEEN A UNIVERSITY & COLLEGE

Before we even dip our toe into the Elite application world, we must understand the difference between a University and a College. When a student graduates from high school, the next step is to either attend a 2-year Community College that will offer an Associate Degree or attend a 4-year undergraduate University or College that offers a bachelor's degree (BA) in the Arts and/or Sciences.

A **University**, as opposed to a College, is composed of several schools or Colleges, each of which focus on specific areas of studies. In addition to an extensive Undergraduate Program, a University also provides Graduate Programs that offer a wide array of Professional Degrees. The University's combined Undergraduate and Graduate student population can be large. This community will also often boast extensive athletic programs, clubs, organizations, research programs, and the like.

A **College**, while like a University, offers limited options when it comes to fields of study, and typically does not offer master's programs. Throughout this book I will use the word "Schools" as a universal term when referring the application process to both Universities and Colleges.

Applying to and attending either a University or a College is dependent upon the subjective needs of the applicant. I can give you the facts so you and your kid can make the most informed decision possible, but one thing I cannot do in this book is determine whether your kid should apply to a University or a College. This is a personal decision for your student to make.

CHAPTER 3

WHY IS IT SO DAMN DIFFICULT TO GET ACCEPTED TO AN ELITE SCHOOL?

Only one thing is certain when applying to an Elite School…and that one thing is that **nothing** is 'certain.' I hate to be the bearer of bad news, but I feel a responsibility to be the voice of reason. The reality is that each year thousands and thousands of brilliant, over-Qualified high school seniors get rejected, deferred, or waitlisted from Elite Institutions.

An IRL ("In Real Life") example, was where a friend's daughter was so sure she was going to get accepted Early Decision to an Ivy League School ("IVY"), she invited her friends and family to a preemptive celebratory dinner. Then, 'it' happened. She opened the email… I will spare you the gruesome details and just leave it at there were a lot of unhappy people eating Italian food that night. Yes, this girl totally did not expect to be rejected. Sadly, she is not alone.

The truth is that most qualified students believe in earnest that their acceptance is a clear slam-dunk, and then when it is not, they are left clueless and in tears with no backup plan except wallowing in self-pity.

After meandering through the application process under the assumption they will absolutely be admitted only to discover the words 'We are sorry to inform you…' in their inbox, parents and kids find themselves in an unthinkable position—they are forced to change or lower their expectations. #SAD.

The application process is this *hyper-competitive.*

Each year, high school seniors submit their applications to the Elite Institutions they *believed* they were destined to attend. They confidently swaggered among their peers in the school hallways, wearing the Elite School sweatshirt (HUGE MISTAKE), and WHAM! Slammed with a rejection letter, which came out of nowhere. Yes, this kid totally did not expect to get rejected.

It happens just like that! One minute you and your kid believe, in earnest, that it is a slam dunk he or she will get accepted, and the next minute you both are in tears, lost, no back up plan, clueless and wallowing in self-pity. Not to mention that the previously purchased 'Elite' gear, that cost a small fortune, was ripped to shreds and thrown out in pure disgust (by both the kid and the parent).

Most of the kids that get rejected or deferred, along with their parents, meandered through the application process with the presumption that they would absolutely wind up in the 'admit' pile. These kids go on social media to find their only consolation prize is that many of their friends have shared a similar fate. Do not even get me started on what happens when these kids, find out which classmates *were* accepted to their dream school.

The emotional breakdown lasts for days, wherein a debate ensues as to the *legitimacy* of the other acceptances. Yes, you heard me. There is 'catfighting', where the rejected kids question the qualifications of the *accepted* students. Let's talk real terms: classmates go for the jugular and want to know *how* a kid 'got in'. Varsity Blues brings this line of inquiry to a new low, for the reasons that have been set forth in the criminal indictment. Regardless, the rejected kid must move on...

Wake up and smell the roses, my fellow parents. Your kid might be deferred, waitlisted, or rejected from all the Elite Schools they applied to. You both need to be ready to lace up your tennis shoes and get on the rebound.

By that I mean you need to be prepared to apply to the Middle Tier Schools. Please take a deep breath, as there is no shame in applying to the non-designer label Schools. Yes, crazy parents, there are other Schools out there to consider. The next level of Schools, the 'Middle Tier' is not a banishment, or failure. Quite the contrary.

REMEMBER: It is not about you.

I can empathize with the heartbreak parents feel alongside their kids. The emotional breakdown experienced by your kid, is understandable. I have watched kids read their decision letters. It is incredible to observe their face, which is covered with stress induced acne, dramatically change when excited anticipation turns to despondency while reading a rejection letter(s). Please note the plural, yes, there can be more than one. This #SUCKS.

What follows next are the tears, the high-pitched shrieks, the bedroom door slam, and finally, the sulking for days on end... Yes, rock bottom depression.

Why such drama? All applicants believe the rejection letter defined them as #NOTGOODENOUGH.

I will let you in on a secret... plenty of 'good enough' kids will get rejection letters. Many kids who are rejected boast stellar credentials and are super-stars in and out of the classroom. Yet they still get rejected from the Elite Schools they aspired to attend.

They all ask the same question: What was wrong with their seemingly perfect application? Even worse, when they ask... "What is wrong with me?". That second question is counterproductive, not to mention, a real heart wrench-ing, demoralizing moment.

#WISEWORDS: We all know there is nothing 'wrong' with the applicant and they should not perceive themselves as less intelligent or less of a person. Please re-read this statement, because it is profound and the truth.

REASONS WHY IT SO DIFFICULT TO GET ACCEPTED

1. Admission Rules Differ from Year to Year

The Qualified, Compelling, now rejected applicant appeared to have all the right stuff. They marched in lockstep and complied with everything their guidance counselors, teachers, College advisors, and parents told them to do. They subjected themselves to the hardest curriculum offered at their respective high school, received stellar grades, and participated in Extraordinary Extracurricular Activities ("EC's") like a 'Rock Star'. They played the College-application-game well and followed every rule as it was given to them.

What more could the Dean *want*? What stone was left unturned?

As you know, there is a greater concentration of exceptional applicants each new admission cycle. In response to the demand of highly Qualified applicants, each year the Dean revises the admission requirements that are implemented to accept, reject, defer, or waitlist students.

With the 'rules' changing each year, it's impossible for an aspiring applicant to know exactly what the Dean wants. So, if you were planning to mold your kid into the cookie-cutter shape of the 'perfect applicant' that is predicated on the previous year's admission cycle, that strategy will #FAIL.

2. Overabundance of Qualified Applicants

Despite the high price tag that comes with attending a four-year Elite Institution, applications to these Schools are increasing exponentially. Each year, tens of thousands of more students apply to these coveted institutions. The more the merrier, right? Wrong.

The Deans of Undergraduate Admissions at Elite Schools are not pleased with these statistics. Why? As it stands now, the overabundance of Qualified applicants is so great that Deans could fill the size of at least three, full first-year classes each admissions cycle.

No Dean wants to deny a Qualified applicant the opportunity to be educated at their Elite School, but there are physically just not enough first-year seats available to meet the growing demand.

In many ways, it would seem that many Elite Institutions embrace this demand to their own benefit. The lower the admissions rate, the higher the school's rankings and, thus, the more applicants vying for one of the few coveted spots in the incoming first-year class. This cycle of exclusivity is self-perpetuating. Higher rankings lead to more applicants, which causes lower acceptance rates, which leads to higher rankings, and on and on...

It is not a very big leap to imagine that the Board of Trustees are praising the Dean for the aura of exclusivity and prestige that their institution comes to portray on the international stage because of this growing selectivity. Everyone wants to be linked to a prestigious College or University in one way or another, and fundraising dollars are as good a link as any.

Applying to these bastions of academia is easy... the hard part is getting #ACCEPTED. I have been exactly where you are now, deep in the complex, and often contradictory, world of helping students apply to Elite Institutions.

At the end of that final traumatic school year, where seniors are rejected from the school of their dreams, parents chant the same, sad dirge... *"I wish I knew then what I know now."* I do not want you, my fellow parent to say that.

If you follow this book as a guide, not just to an Elite acceptance, but to parenting at large, chances are you will bypass the dreaded words *'woulda'*, *'coulda'*, *'shoulda'*.

The key to avoiding the Monday-morning-quarterback-trap is #PREPARATION. Aspiring applicants and their parents are often misinformed as how to navigate the Elite admissions process. The biggest mistake they make: 1. Have no plan and 2. They start to think about the College process too late.

11th grade is too late. 12th grade is *way* too late.

Turns out, like anything good in life, *preparing* your kid to be a competitive Elite applicant takes time, and years of #FUTUREPLANNING.

I am not here to tell you how to parent... that is your business. What I will tell you is that based on my personal experience of choosing to be that all-in 'crazy' parent who monitors their kid's intellectual and academic development, I've learned a lot about how our system of education works in this country.

Nurturing a child to have the curiosity and self-awareness of their own intellectual prowess that is necessary to take accountability for their own destiny is a lengthy process.

But do not fear. If you start small, and start *soon*, you will be well on your way to raising a uniquely Qualified Elite applicant… and a pretty *cool* person, too.

CHAPTER 4

WHY YOUR KID WILL GET REJECTED!

Such a downer to start a chapter, right? What can I say? I am candid. To be blunt, which you may have gathered is my style by now, most parents and their spawn are ignorant to the complexity inherent in applying to an Elite Institution.

Everyone wants their kids to attend an Elite School, but few understand the multi-year commitment it takes to *prepare* a kid to become an Elite applicant. Your kid's senior year of high school is too late to prepare to apply to an Elite School. Honey, that ship sailed a long time ago and everyone on it is waving from the dock chanting 'you missed the boat'!

In my house, the odyssey of molding my kids towards becoming superior students and extraordinary people started at birth. I kid you not.

Joking aside, Kids are #BRAINWASHED that they will attend an Elite College and/or University at an early age. They are educated in a rigorous academic environment; expectations are high, and over time they are expected to acquire the skills to be a Qualified applicant and assume responsibility for their work product and future academic destiny.

If your kids aspire to attend an Elite School, they must take *ownership* for their academics, grades, and participation. Parents cannot do their kids homework and projects. Well, maybe it is okay to make that collage of the solar system when they are in 2nd grade because you will have more fun creating that work of art!

What parents can do, is to make it your mission to put all the pieces into place to facilitate their journey for future success. Buckle up! This is no easy task.

You are in it for the #LONGHAUL.

First things first, you need to educate *yourself*. Knowing the pitfalls most parents and kids slip into during the Elite application process is the first step to avoiding them. As we move through this chapter, I identify the "Top Five Common Reasons for Rejection", as well as provide an IRL example, that we can all learn from...

THE TOP FIVE MOST COMMON REASONS FOR REJECTION!

Drum roll please!

1) REJECTION: Longshot to Get Accepted

I cannot seem to say it enough... Anyone can apply to Elite Institutions, that is a mere formality, the hard part is getting accepted. Based on current odds, the chances of most students getting Accepted are slim to none. If you are feeling 'lucky,' you might have a better time at Vegas. Most students will get rejected from every Elite School to which they apply. #COLDHARDTRUTH.

#WISEWORDS: Acceptance to an Elite School is a #LONGSHOT for *every* applicant, there are #NOGUARANTEES.

Oh, to the contrary, we have all learned that some parents do not want their kid to be a 'long shot,' but opt for a guaranteed 'sure bet' admission. #VARSITYBLUES.

As you are aware, these parents re-defined the current competitive application environment and turned it on its head when 50 people were indicted in the largest U.S. College Admissions Bribery Scandal.

A review of the indictment, which revealed countless pages of wiretapped telephone conversations, alleged parents intentionally leveraged their prestige, power, and substantial wealth to completely alter the legitimacy of the College application process.

According to the indictment, these parents knew their kids did not satisfy the College admission requirements and paid copious amounts of money to bribe a variety of standardized test proctors and College and/or University athletic coaches to *guarantee* their kid's admission.

Well now, that is unbelievable. #RIGGEDSYSTEM.

In the old days, that is to say, the day before the Varsity Blues indictment was unsealed, the most outrageous thing wealthy or famous parents would do was to legitimately donate large sums of money to the College of their choosing in a vain attempt to secure an acceptance. In this scenario, the applicant's chances for admission would most likely increase, although would still not be a guarantee for admission. The applicant must still meet the minimum admission requirements.

To be clear, these were and continue to be lawful donations made directly to the school, with the intent to be used for the betterment of the College or University. These are donations, not bribes. There is no quid pro quo.

On the other hand, according to the indictment, Varsity Blues was a scheme, devised to have key people who themselves were knowing participants, located throughout the admissions food chain with the intent to corrupt the college admission system by accepting bribes in exchange for a guaranteed admission ticket.

Even though their kids failed to meet the admission qualifications of test scores and EC's, the indictment meticulously set forth how each of these parents participated in a coordinated effort, a scheme, that either altered standardized test scores or forged their child's status as a student athlete in spite of the fact that their child had never played said sport!

The Colleges and/or Universities apparently did not benefit from these illicit transactions. Another reason for such a huge public outcry: Was it just cheaper to pay a bribe to secure a guaranteed Acceptance, rather than donate directly to the Institution where there would be no guaranteed acceptance?

VARSITY BLUES revealed a new generation of parent— the truly *desperate* parent. In fact, in one broad stroke, these parents re-defined the 'desperate parent' by allegedly breaking the law. FYI, I am constantly re-editing this book because one parent just pled guilty.

These desperate parents eclipsed your garden variety of crazy parents, because they wanted that acceptance, that slam-dunk, at any cost.

Here is a novel concept— students are accepted to an Elite School because they earned it; years of achieving outstanding grades in rigorous academic courses and receiving high standardized test scores. These were the real victims of the Varsity Blue Scam. In many ways, it can be asserted that the Varsity Blues parents bought a first-Year seat at an Elite School for their less qualified kids. They stole a seat from a Qualified Compelling Applicant, who earned that seat.

We hope Varsity Blues is the rare exception rather than the new rule of how to get an acceptance letter in your mailbox. The facts are that even alumni and donors are not sure bets these days. It is that competitive. For the rest of us mere mortals, the odds are against the student seeking to gain admission. They will always be a #LONGSHOT.

REMEMBER: An adolescent must earn accomplishments, not be given them. A child does not profit from being handed accolades.

#WISEWORDS: I am jail-averse, and at the end of the day, is it really that important to bribe, steal, and cheat to get your kid accepted to an Elite School? #HELLNO.

#WISEWORDS: DO make sure your kid satisfies the requirements for admission with top grades, scores, and extraordinary EC's. If you hire people to take your kid's standardized tests and lie about their activities, the current reality is that you just might succumb to a fate similar to the Varsity Blues parents.

2)REJECTION:Greater Demand=Lower Admit Rate

Truly understanding the admissions process is a daunting task. The global demand for acceptance to an Elite School absolutely outweighs the availability of spots. I cannot reiterate this enough, even though I have talked about this ad nauseum!

The reality is that every new admissions cycle eclipses the previous year for total applicants. You are not alone in asking, "Why is this happening?"

The trend over the last decade has been that more Qualified high school seniors are applying to Elite Schools because they share the fantasy of getting accepted. Everyone wants to attend these schools.

The applicant pool is growing exponentially, and yet the number of spots in each first-year class stays the same. Because of this, the acceptance rate, or 'yield,' for Elite Schools gets lower each year, narrowing the window for Qualified, Compelling applicants to receive acceptances from the Elite School of their choosing.

Despite this current competitive application environment, students continue to be compelled to apply to these Elite Schools that boast exceptionally low admit rates.

What is the attraction to Elite Schools in the first place? Social media, movies, parents, and society at large are all responsible for creating this frenzied demand. Everybody seems to want that Designer Label School, which evokes those 'gotta have it' feelings.

We parents place the kids who are accepted to, and subsequently attend these Elite Schools on pedestals. We act awestruck by their mere presence, drop to the floor, and hyperventilate just knowing this kid will attend that Elite School.

Clearly, I am blowing this totally out of proportion, and even though we do not behave that way in public, we will do so in the privacy of our own home!

In truth, the kids who got accepted to an Elite School beat the odds. We are facing admit rates of 3 to 9%, which makes it quite realistic that even the most compelling applicant will get rejected. This is another reason why kids apply to Elite Schools—facing insurmountable odds, impressionable kids and parents all want what they cannot have. #HUMANNATURE

In our society, where profound wealth and power rests in the top one-tenth of the 1%, parents look at Elite institutions as an opportunity to jettison their kids towards unfathomable success. These regaled institutions are considered a bastion for the societal elite. Historically, they have been held in the highest esteem throughout the world.

It is no surprise that applicants are climbing over each other for a chance to become a lifetime member of that prestigious club. But the insatiable demand for these Elite Institutions is having a deleterious effect on the ability of future applicants to secure an acceptance.

The admit rate continues to get lower with each new annual admissions cycle. Soon, any opportunity of acceptance will be virtually extinguished because the demand has continued to grow despite the staggering amount of rejections received by applicants each year.

This is a vicious cycle, and, unfortunately, there seems to be no end in sight.

The low acceptance rate has become an unintended consequence of this growing annual application parade.

As if you needed one more reminder IRL to exemplify this 'Elite College Crisis,' here you go... About 5 years ago, an Elite University admission's rate dipped below 5% for the first time in history. Now, more Schools are in step with that rate, which is unwelcome news for applicants.

In fact, each high school senior who was not accepted Early Decision to an Elite School, will submit an average of 20-25 regular decision College applications, many of which overlap the same Elite Schools. Hmmm. Are you starting to understand why the number of applicants to Elite Schools increase exponentially?

As a parent, step back for a moment. It has become all too common for high school seniors to submit an excessive number of applications because they know they will get rejected from most, if not all, of the Elite Schools. So why are we allowing this? What is the point?

These kids understand that there is a remarkably high probability they will get rejected, and yet everyone thinks there is that 'chance' that he or she will be accepted. I understand that no one wants to feel like they are closing the door on the possible 'opportunity of a lifetime'. The truth is, based on the sheer numbers we have already addressed, it can be a #WASTEOFTIME.

3) REJECTION: Failure to Have Superior Grades & Standardized Test Scores

#ROUND-ONE of the admission process requires an applicant to have top grades and board scores. Failure to meet this requirement results in rejection in the First Round of review by the Admissions Committee. When parents and students begin to research Elite Schools, everyone automatically presumes that a straight 'A' average and perfect board scores guarantees admission. However, parents must be aware that while it is fantastic if their kid has straight 'A's in all their AP courses, that's just #ROUND-ONE.

Tens of thousands of Qualified applicants to these Elite Schools are 'perfect' on paper.

REMEMBER: If an applicant does not have stellar grades and standardized scores that meet the minimum requirement for admission, you are out of the running from the starting line.

4) REJECTION: Failure to Display Extraordinary Qualities

Welcome to #ROUND-TWO of the Admissions process. In this Round, the Dean of Undergraduate Admission asks one simple question: *'Show Me What Else You Have Done.'* If you believed that grades and scores were all you needed to get into an Elite School, now is the time to realize you are sadly mistaken. Photoshopping your kid's head onto another high school soccer player's body does not prove your kid is Extraordinary.

5) REJECTION: Learn from Other Rejected Applicants

Kids become aware of the application process in 10th grade, when they watch the seniors apply to Elite Schools, and receive their acceptance and/or rejection letters. The seniors are irrationally confident they will get accepted to their number one choice and, of course, their second, third, and fourth choice Colleges as well. These seniors, many whom were in the top of their class, appeared to be the *perfect applicant.*

#REALITY sets in when the seniors receive their decision letters. News travels fast. One or two kids get accepted to only one Elite School. The news on Decision day only gets worse. They learn that most of the top students were rejected from their first choices, while other classmates did not get accepted to any of their top 5 choice schools. These kids are in a state of shock, saying it 'can't be true they were rejected', and of course, lamenting this was 'a total surprise'.

REMEMBER: Top grades and high board scores are not enough to secure admission.

REMEMBER: It is a #LONGSHOT for a Qualified applicant to get accepted to an Elite School.

REMEMBER: An applicant must be QUALIFIED, ENGAGED and COMPELLING to make it to the final admission rounds. Then you pray for the coveted acceptance to an Elite Institution.

The chilling reality sets in that the next kid, your kid, who has a flawless academic record, just might, get rejected from every Elite School to which they apply. I know, you are in panic mode.

So, what do you do? You read this book. Ignorance is not bliss. Ignorance is not a defense in a criminal case, nor is it an excuse for not getting your kid into an

Elite College or University.

#WISEWORDS: #FUTUREPLANNING #PREPARATION.

I was, and remain, that 'crazy parent' who went to the ends of this earth (and back again) to help send my kids to an Elite School. At my first Elite application rodeo with my eldest son, I knew that it would be a formidable challenge, a #LONGSHOT.

To meet the challenge head on, I assembled a team of College advisors to provide guidance throughout this process and ask questions. This is key. In addition to frequently speaking with these 'experts,' I also read books, searched the internet, in my vain attempts to glean tidbits of information to understand the Elite application process.

The competitive part of me wanted to 'game it.' By 'game it,' I meant that I wanted to understand the rules and requirements necessary to play the Elite admissions game, that would make my kids legitimate Qualified, competitive applicants. My interpretation of 'gaming it' was to encourage my sons to follow their dreams. The pursuit of their dreams was synonymous with Passion, which was exemplified and evidenced by EC's. This resulted in them both considered 'Compelling applicants' by Admissions.

Our dear VARSITY BLUES Parents, on the other hand, had quite a different understanding of the term 'game.' These parents seemingly knew that their kids did not meet the requirements for admission, but rather than find different Colleges and/or Universities that would complement their kids' individual skill sets, as alleged in the indictment, they embarked on a journey to manipulate standardized test scores and personal information. That is not 'gaming,' it is just flat-out cheating. #DON'TDOIT.

I found the application process fascinating because it was and continues to be wildly unpredictable. My unwavering tenacity to master the application process at times proved fruitful that I often found myself sharing information I gleaned with the 'professionals' who were advising my son.

Despite all my efforts, my friends and I were still newbies when it came to apply our kids to Schools. None of us knew what to do and, in truth, we learned that many College advisors were not too helpful either. We consistently received inconsistent information regarding the application process, and that was understandably problematic.

Everyone made mistakes and was susceptible to getting wrong advice. When the rejections, waitlists, and deferrals came in our kids were all heartbroken, miserable, and depressed. It was a truly horrible time in all our lives, not to mention it was the start of the holiday season, and there would be no HO-HO -HO's. It was, as my kids say, a #SHITSHOW.

It is extremely hard to deal with disappointment, for both the student and parent. This is especially true when you and your kid had unrealistic expect- ations that they had any chance of getting accepted in the first place.

As we discussed, you must be fast on the rebound. Rather than wallow in a pity-party, I threw myself back into understanding how the College applica- tion process worked with even greater fervor than before. My friends and fel- low parents laughed at me, and thought I was wasting my time trying to figure out how to get kids into Elite Schools.

Laugh all you want – it was and remains that important to me. We are all mo- ments away from becoming a desperate parent, grasping to find any support that will act as that extra boost to get our kids into their dream school.

It is paramount to stay ahead of the game, stay informed, and stay open to cul- tivating your kid's Passion and Intellectual Potential.

IRL Example: Real Life Fiasco of an Early Decision Application.

The following is a true story. This is not unique, happens to many applicants. The takeaway is to learn from the rejections. #BEWARNED!

This scenario happens all too often, because students do not understand the application process. In this case, "Craig" applied Early Decision (ED) to an Ivy League School (IVY). This was his dream school, and he convinced himself he was a 'shoe in' to get accepted. He even bought an IVY sweatshirt that he wore every day #BIGMISTAKE #JINX.

Craig believed he would get accepted because he had strong standardized test scores, great GPA, and, wait for it, he was the Captain of the school Robot- ics Team. I laugh as I write this, not to be mean, but because even though it sounds like a big accomplishment, it bears minimal significance. Elite Col- leges and Universities really do not care. Sorry to be so harsh, but it is true.

Later in this book you will learn how to effectively parlay these types of Leadership roles and EC's in the applicant's personal story. See Chapters 20-23.

When a kid is a captain of any team, it is something that gets thrown onto the leadership pile for EC's on the application. However, the odds that this will be the thing to tip the scale and get you into an Elite school are slim to none. "Why is this?" you ask. Simple. Because most Qualified applicants have done everything but find the cure for cancer.

"ED" day typically falls on December 15th, although some schools will report their decisions earlier. On December 15th, Craig learned his fate. Let us take bets now—do you think he was accepted or rejected? If you answered 'yes' to either choice, you were wrong. He got 'Deferred.' None of us understood what that meant. We took out our phones and typed into google: "meaning of deferment from an Elite ED round." We were just clueless as to what should be the next step for Craig.

This kid had entered the proverbial 'twilight zone' of Elite admissions. Not rejected, not accepted, just deferred. After months of torturing himself over deciding where to apply and when, he was here, there, and nowhere.

Craig's application would be tossed into the Regular Admission ("RA") pool, where he would have little to no chance of getting accepted. Why do I have such a doom and gloom attitude? Here is the answer: When a student applies to an Elite School in the RA application pool, they must go up against all the brilliant kids who chose to apply RA to this school, in addition to all the students who were rejected from the other Elite Schools they applied to ED.

FYI, the kids who were rejected or deferred from their Elite ED Schools, throw their applications into the RA pool of every Elite School to see what will 'stick'. Thus, the application numbers to these Elite Schools increase by the tens of thousands once you enter the RA pool. This lowers the odds to get accepted.

This #SUCKS. It really does, and that is why the applicant and their entourage must know what the Dean wants and understand how to apply to an Elite School. #PREACHTOCHOIR.

Getting back to Craig. Poor, poor Craig was totally lost because he had no back up plan. He was so convinced he would get accepted to that IVY, his number one and only, it never occurred to him to make any alternative plans.

#WISEWORDS: When you apply ED, you always need a #BACKUPPLAN.

Most kids do not have a BACKUPPLAN.

#YOUARESCREWED.

And by the way. Craig's situation is not unique. So many smart kids, have walked, are walking, or will walk in Craig's shoes.

Let's get back to Craig, who had a real problem... He had to pick other Colleges to which he would apply, none of which he wanted to attend. He also had to deal with the imminent regular decision deadline, which is always January 1st. Submitting new application(s) is not easy, because each Elite School requests additional essays to be written as supplements to the Common Application ("Common App"). This is a time intensive task. We will discuss the Common App in Chapter 22.

Craig had just 2 weeks to pull himself together and slap himself back into the reality of finding other Colleges and/or Universities to apply to... during the holiday season of all times. I can assure you that the house of a deferred or rejected student is not brimming with holiday spirit. There is no time to spare. #LIFEGOESON.

The BAD NEWS for Craig, was that all the college advisors, and guidance counselors are either on vacation or will be on vacation. The rejected or deferred kid, Craig in this instant, was on his own. #OHSHIT!

The GOOD NEWS for Craig, he already had a completed Common App, essays, and resume.

The BAD NEWS was that all the Elite School forms and essays looked like a 5-year-old applied to the IVY. I kid you not. There were so many things that needed to be done, and there was no time. Everyone was going away on vacation in just a few days and Craig had to dramatically revise his Common App. 'Revise' was a gentle way of saying the entire Common App needed to be completely re-written.

For a high school student, Craig was a highly intelligent, inquisitive, independent thinker, whose life was consumed with entrepreneurship, engineering, and robotics. He aspired to develop robotic technology that would be implemented throughout all aspects of industry. Unfortunately, these impressive goals were in no way, shape or form conveyed to the IVY.

Unbeknownst to Craig, he extinguished any chance he had to get accepted in the ED round because he failed to define and portray himself as a Qualified, Engaged and Compelling applicant.

#WISEWORDS: All applicants to Elite Institutions must hit a home run when they tell their personal story and figuratively leap off the pages to the Dean of Undergraduate Admissions.

In my heart of hearts, there is absolutely no rhyme or reason as to how or why certain smart kids wind up at Elite Schools while others do not. There are way too many Qualified and over-Qualified kids that get rejected from Elite Schools and not enough first-year seats. #BASICMATH

As a parent, you can twist yourself into a million pieces to do the right thing for your kid and try to give them every opportunity to help them have an edge in life. When it comes to applying to Elite Schools, there are simply #NOGUARANTEES.

Once again, an applicant needs to know what the Dean wants and understand how the admission process works. I know, I know, I keep saying this over and over. This knowledge will either make the #ACCEPTANCE sweeter or lessen the agony of the #REJECTION.

REMEMBER: It is common for parents to be more disappointed with a rejection, than their kid. You were the one who structured their life path to lead to perceived success you thought started with an acceptance letter from an Elite Institution. They did not get in, and now there is nothing you can do.... Or is there?

CHAPTER 5

HOW TO LEGITIMATELY IMPROVE THE ODDS WHEN THE DECK IS STACKED AGAINST AN APPLICANT

Welcome to the 21st Century of applying to an Elite Schools. The Elite U.S. Academic Institutions can receive upwards of **40,000** applications for its first-year class admissions cycle. This number varies from School to School, but still reflects an upward tick of applicants.

If you can believe this, an Elite Public University received over 111,000 applicants for the first-year class admission cycle in 2019. To put this in perspective, in 2015 this same University received 93,000 applicants.

The increase in applications to all Elite Schools has been increasing exponentially each admissions cycle, with no downtick in sight. These numbers blow my mind. I have been writing this book for the last few years, and I continually upwardly revise the application number, which is crazy.

It is clear that from a numbers' standpoint, the demand to attend an Elite School is highly competitive. Thus, even when your kid is smart, high achieving, and multi-talented, all parents must have *reasonable* expectations that the odds are still against your kid getting accepted #LONGSHOT.

As we have discussed, these odds can make parents crazy, and worse, create the *desperate parent.* #VARSITYBLUES.

This is where my fellow parents need to pay attention. #HEADSUP! To improve the odds for acceptance, **you must know *HOW* to apply your kid *legit-***

imately and lawfully **to an Elite School.**

Applying to Elite Schools is a marathon that starts when your child is born. I am not joking. For the highly intelligent, high-achieving student, it is too late to first talk about attending these schools with your child in their junior year of high school. Honey, I already told you, that ship sailed a long time ago...

This book provides an informal timeline as how to best prepare your *smart* kid to be a Qualified *and* Compelling applicant to an Elite U.S. Academic Institution. The key throughout this entire process is to understand as a parent, how to raise, or better yet, brainwash your kid to be a Qualified and Compelling applicant.

If the goal is for your kid to attend an Elite School, you will know by the time they are a rising high school senior whether he or she is not only Qualified, but a Compelling applicant. You *should* know, because you have been working towards this goal for the last 17 out of 17 years of your kid's life!

The real problem is that most of these kids should not be applying to Elite Schools in the first place. Yes, you heard me. Most of the kids who apply to Elite Schools are not Qualified applicants.

These Elite schools are 'reach' schools and are not within their reach. Many applicants disregard the Schools' detailed requirements for admission. In many regards, it takes years to meet the minimum requirements.

Here is a novel concept, that I am sure many parents do not think when their kid is poised to apply to College. Critical to the success of any adolescent, is whether the kid is happy and socially adjusted among peers. As a parent, did you ever wonder if your kid is happy? A child will not achieve academically and reach their intellectual potential in the absence of happiness and emotional stability.

Additionally, when a child is happy, they will thrive on an intellectual level, and thus be guided to the best Schools that compliment who they are as people. Elite Schools are comprised of an intelligent, motivated, and intellectually curious student body.

If your kid is a not a Qualified applicant, the Elite Schools they apply to may not be the right kind of environment for your kid's academic and emotional well-being.

Did you ever think the academics at the Elite Schools are incredibly challenging, tailor made for a highly intelligent student body? Be sensitive to their needs and do not overplay your hand. You as a parent, may want your kid to attend an Elite School, but it just might not in the best interest of your kid.

Seriously, I implore you all to throw away the #ROSE-COLORED GLASSES (or 'Designer' glasses) we all wear when we look at our kids. See them for who they are as people, with their warts and all, and guide them to be the best they can be.

When I was raising my kids, I kept the bar extremely high for achievement, because I knew what they could achieve, while understanding their limitations. Thus, when I pushed my kids to take that extra step to achieve, I would ask them "Why be ordinary when you can be Extraordinary?"

I maintain that kids should want to be #EXTRAORDINARY. Extraordinary is not measured by how much money your kid will make, or how many followers they have on twitter, but by how they choose to make a positive impact in their community, or selflessly improve the lives of others #KINDNESS.

CHAPTER 6

RAISE YOUR KID TO BE A
QUALIFIED APPLICANT

A Qualified applicant is a high school senior who is in the top 5% of their graduating class, has a stunning transcript replete with all the required coursework, high if not *perfect* standardized board scores (The SAT or ACT), and extensive EC's that distinguish them from other applicants.

I'm speaking directly to the parents that have always had their proverbial hand in the pot with their kids a.k.a. the 'Tiger Moms', 'Overbearing Moms' and 'Helicopter Parents.'

You all know who you are, and we all know that most of your kids are not merely led to water and left alone to drink. Rather, they are dragged, kicking, and screaming, along the way. Regardless of any negatively charged moniker, we moms have tried in earnest to position our kids' lives for only positive outcomes. We are adamant there is no room for failure.

THE ROSE-COLORED GLASS SYNDROME:
PARENTS MUST REALISTICALLY SEE
THEIR KIDS FOR WHO THEY ARE!

Parents and their kids are *unrealistic* when they begin the College search. Due to ignorance, they start looking at Schools that are simply 'out of their league'. #DELUSIONAL. Meaning, their kid is not a Qualified applicant to the Elite Schools they are considering.

I can make this outrageous statement because I have rubbed elbows with countless over-zealous families from both coasts of this country, all of whom are desperate to get their kid into an Elite School.

Most of these families are unaware that the Dean of Undergraduate Admissions sets forth the requirements to be a Qualified Applicant. I know this sounds harsh, but it is imperative that at the beginning of a College search, the applicant must know whether he or she meets the Dean's *definition* of a Qualified Applicant.

Throughout the years, I have seen countless families reach beyond the stars when they look at Elite Schools. These parents actually 'see stars' when they look at their kids. They genuinely believe their kids will get into the school of their dreams because they perceive their offspring are geniuses that are the 'best' at everything.

Better yet, most parents feel their kid deserves to be accepted, because he or she is a 'good kid' and 'works so hard.'

I am speaking directly to you now... yes, *you*. You know you are guilty of making at least one, if not all, of these statements. And I am guilty to of all the above.

I once attended an admissions event hosted by an Elite School, that of course, will go unnamed. I was talking with a high school senior and her mom. I asked the student if she would be applying to *this* school and the mom perked up, quickly brushed aside her daughter and began to rattle off the names of 5 other Elite schools to which she was confident her daughter would apply and be accepted. Oh, and the daughter also believed she was a 'shoe-in' to get accepted to any Elite School she applied to. Wow... isn't that special! I laughed to myself. Did she not know anyone could recite a memorized list of Elite Schools?

However, this scenario paled in comparison to my next encounter with the overconfident. I met another mom who was boasting about her son. And he, in turn, boasted about himself. How sweet and cyclical. They both were bursting with an absolute aura of confidence that he was the perfect candidate and there was unequivocally no doubt that he would get accepted to a certain Elite School. In their minds, both mom and son were convinced he met every admission requirement.

I could not help but think what a disservice this mother was doing to her

child allowing (and encouraging!) him to think like that when, in truth, there are
#NOGUARANTEES.

As the saying goes, reality bites. The above real-life examples are classic cases of parents who are overly confident that Elite Schools are just opening their doors and rolling out the red carpet for their kids.

CHAPTER 7

CAN YOU GAME THE SYSTEM BY SENDING KIDS TO PRIVATE SCHOOL?

L et us face it, many parents, if they can afford it, will choose to send their kids solely to private school. There is a calculated reason for this, and it is not for the school to become a country club for parents.

The crazy truth is that the frenzied race to attend an elite Schools begins not in high school, but in *nursery school*. The dramatic music should queue in now...

WARNING: Savvy parents are vying for coveted spots to elite private nursery schools when their kids are just two years old. Yes, you heard me correctly, *Two. Years. Old.* Do you sense the level of desperation that envelops these parents?

PARENTS WANT THAT 'EDGE'

These Nursery school parents were savvy. Their kids received their first acceptance to an Elite School when they were just 3 years old. The parents had insight into the crazy College process that was 15 years down the road.

They had that same mommy crystal ball and looked to the future to guide their present decisions. These parents are well educated, accomplished, and somehow knew that starting their toddler at an Elite Nursery School would *begin* the upward trajectory to an Elite College or University.

These parents also knew that Elite private high schools traditionally sent a percentage of each graduating class to Elite Colleges. That is one reason why they chose to send their kids only to private schools. They wanted to *secure* that *#EDGE*.

The Deans at Elite Colleges and/or Universities are very familiar with these high schools, specifically their rigorous curriculum, academic expectations, and the type of student these schools 'pump out' each year.

Traditionally, Elite Colleges 'set aside' several first-year seats for Elite private high schools. Yes, they have been considered Feeder schools. These high schools have proven track records of their graduates' academic qualifications, and success as a college student at not only their respective Elite Colleges, but all of them.

Historically, Elite private high schools throughout the U.S. have fed approximately 2-5 Qualified, Compelling graduating seniors to *each* Elite University and/or College every admission cycle.

Sending your kid to an Elite private school *has been* a legitimate attempt to game the system. Please note the 'past tense' of the previous sentence.

Of course, there is a problem with this plan to send kids to private high schools. What? This angle may not work anymore? As you know, nothing stays the same.

In our *current* hyped-up Elite admissions process, parents are finding it harder and harder every year to 'game the system'. #NOGUARANTEES.

There are a finite number of seats in each entering first-year class, and this number remains constant... Elite Schools do not add seats.

There are years when private schools do not get a high number of students accepted to Elite Schools. #WTF?! You can imagine how this totally pisses off so many parents, not to mention their kids.

These parents fully comprehend how difficult it is for kids to get into Elite Colleges—they know there are not enough first-year seats.

The problem for private school students, is that many public high schools are also on the Dean's radar. Thus, thousands upon thousands, upon thousands of highly intelligent, accomplished, overly Qualified public-school students are also competing for an acceptance.

I totally understand, I am making your head spin. In addition to U.S. applicants, do not forget about the global demand of international students who also want to attend these Elite institutions.

Now our heads are exploding. This means more applicants, not enough first year seats, and the realization that life is just #NOTFAIR.

CHAPTER 8

THE IMPORTANCE OF ACADEMICS THROUGHOUT THE MIDDLE YEARS

Personally, I believe there is a misnomer as to how people classify intellectual ability, academic achievement, and its effect on creativity. Each child has their own strengths and weaknesses. Barring any physical or emotional limitation that affects cognitive development, I maintain that every child can excel in an academic setting. This is not wishful thinking on my part, but in fact depends upon the belief that children can commit to putting in a lot of hard work.

IT TAKES A VILLAGE...

For students who aspire to attend an Elite School, it can take a village to achieve that goal. In today's world, a parent cannot solely rely on a school to educate their child, nor can a parent rely solely on themselves to raise their kid. Period. End of discussion. We all need #HELP from others.

To attain the goal of an Elite acceptance, a realistic strategy for this achievement should start to be formulated when the student enters middle school. The Middle School Years are emphasized in this book because they are a time when so many life-changing events converge at once for our children. These years can be #TRANSFORMATIVE.

For some children, the transition from elementary school to middle school is significant for several reasons. The children are educated in a more formal academic structure, and expectations are higher. Concurrently, this is when our cute children become teenagers. Heaven help us all.

On a physiological level, hormones are activated, and their little kid bodies slowly morph into adolescent forms. On an emotional level, it is during these years that kids develop a self-awareness of themselves and their place among peers on a social and academic level.

Parental involvement in the emotional and physical development of your child is crucial not only throughout middle school, but through high school as well. In the 21st century, there are so many external pressures, conscious and subconscious, that are placed upon our kids. As parents, we have an obligation to guide our kids through this unchartered territory.

Now, not all parents embrace my views. But regardless of whether you share my parenting philosophy, there is no way around the fact that paramount to the development of our children is their emotional wellbeing.

Let's be realistic. To help a child attain future success on an academic level, we should consciously raise and nurture them to be happy, emotionally and physically healthy, loving, passionate individuals who care not only about the people close to them, but also those in their community and world.

The #HAPPYFACTOR is a key component of who you are and become as a person. If you are not happy, it will be exceedingly difficult to achieve any type of success. This will be discussed at length in Chapter 11.

THE GUIDANCE COUNSELOR

While it may seem early, I highly suggest that prior to the commencement of middle school both parent and child meet with their future Guidance Counselor. This means you would be sitting down with the guidance counselor when your child is in the spring of their 5th grade year.

Since middle school can be a life transition for some children, it is great for our future middle schoolers to know what to expect academically and socially for the fall's upcoming school term.

The guidance counselor can and will provide priceless insight as to how academics are structured at your child's school. Moreover, it is essential that your child develop a *relationship* with his or her counselor.

When a guidance counselor knows your child, they will be able to assess his or her academic abilities and create an individualized academic program that is tailored to your child. #DOTHIS.

This can and does happen at a public school too. What I have learned over the years is that all schools, albeit public or private, educate your child objectively, not subjectively.

What this means is that the high achieving, highly intelligent child does not necessarily receive the academic challenges they require; and/or the child who is struggling may be overlooked and does not receive the assistance they need to overcome their learning struggles.

DUMP AND RUNS ARE NOT PERMITTED!

So, what am I telling you? That a parent cannot just do a #DUMPANDRUN with their kids at school. Ever heard of this phrase? It means you can't dump your kids off at school every day and expect the school to take care of their academic and emotional needs. Forget about it.

Regardless if you are a stay at home parent or working parent, you should #KEEPTABS on your kids 24/7. There is just too much going on in the day and the life of a 21st century middle/high schooler not to be in the #KNOW.

ALWAYS LOOK TO THE FUTURE: THE NEGATIVE IMPACT OF REWARDING FAILURE

Not surprisingly, adolescents at this age get frustrated easily. This can happen when they encounter difficulty in grasping new concepts, enter harder classes, or feel the pressure to meet higher expectations. All these factors can result in lower grades. Since the highly intelligent adolescent will typically be enrolled in all honors courses, I am confident that most if not all these kids will, at some point, be frustrated with learning at an advanced level.

As these smart kids progress through high school, applying to Elite Schools becomes a reality, and the pressure to receive stellar grades can be overwhelming. In truth, at times these kids are under too much pressure to achieve in everything they attempt, namely grades, standardized tests, and EC's.

As a parent, it is crucial for you to be aware of your child's progress in school, and to know if anything might hinder your child from reaching their academic potential. The key to any student's success is for him or her to achieve that which they are capable of. Thus, if a student can achieve personal success in a non-honors math class that corresponds to their ability, then that is wonderful.

Similarly, if a student who tests in the 99% percentile on a math aptitude test is not achieving in an honors math class, the response should *not* be that the child should be moved to a non-honors class.

Oh yes, you heard me.

It is easier to lower the bar, lessen expectations, and have the child *coast* through an easier class.

Moreover, it is easier for the parent to deal with an adolescent who is not frustrated and not angry. Many parents choose to placate their child by taking the easier path. But in the long run, this can be a #MISTAKE.

KIDS MUST LEARN HOW TO COPE
WITH ADVERSITY

It is so important for kids to learn how to deal with failure and #ADVERSITY. This will help them better define who they are as a person in the world... not to mention that the Dean of Undergraduate Admissions wants to know how your son or daughter copes with adversity, too. This will be discussed at length in Chapter 19.

REMEMBER: This book suggests parenting strategies for kids, because your kid's life experiences in grades K-12 do have a profound impact on not only future College choices but on their adult life at large.

So, what is the best advice to give parents when their kid hits that proverbial bump in the road? Most, if not all kids, want to run away from the problem or situation. Yes, it can be a major stress relief for the kid when that problem is just 'taken out' of their life, and it is also easier for the parents, because no one fights. But do you really think you are helping your kid by placating them?

WISEWORDS: Taking the easier path is not a great parental move. *By solving the problem for your kid,* you are not helping your high-achieving child overcome the problem at hand, and you are limiting the development of their skills to deal with adversity in general.

Look at the #BIGPICTURE. When kids are young, every day brings new challenges. They run, they fall, they cry. You teach them how to ride a bike, they fall, they cry. Sometimes they swear they will never get on the bike ever again and they run away. As a parent, your job is to calm your kid down, and then, as the saying goes, get them "back on the horse."

Parents must work to prevent their kid from becoming a #DEFEATIST at an early age. In my opinion, a defeatist is a "Runner Away-er' and this kind of person becomes conditioned to run away from any obstacle. The problem only becomes worse as the kid gets older.

When we allow our kids to 'Run Away', which BTW is *avoidance*, we create a pattern of behavior that #REWARDSFAILURE. We parents certainly do not want to reward failure, but it is so easy to do.

#AMEN, yes, it is. Why do parents get into a pattern of rewarding failure with a teenager? Duh… fewer arguments!

Let's fast forward to high school, so you can understand why rewarding failure does not help any kid. This is an IRL example. Your cute kindergartener, now a high school sophomore, who was always a straight 'A' math student, falls off the proverbial 'cliff' and gets a solid 'C' in math. They are frustrated, because they really do not understand what the disconnect in math is for them.

It is terrible to see your kid feel this way. The frustrations worsen, and the grade does not improve. It becomes important for the parent to intervene, before the problem worsens.

This kid has the simple answer: transfer to a non-honors class ASAP. It might be easy to succumb to this plea. Remember why parents get into a pattern of rewarding failure with a teenager… fewer arguments!

Yes parents, we all prefer fewer arguments with our kids, because it means 3 less gray hairs and a few less scowl lines around our eyes.

Keep in mind, that an easy band-aid solution does not heal the underlying problem. Oh, I am referring to the math class problem. I have to go to the colorist to get rid of the gray, and then hit the dermatologist for a little Botox to freshen up.

All joking aside, what happens if this kid hits another *roadblock* in another honors class? Do you just transfer them out of that class too?

As the parent, it is your job to hold firm and keep the kid in the honors class so they can work through the difficulty. You do not want to create a pattern of behavior where your kid will want to be transferred to an easier class whenever the going gets tough.

This is yet another reason it is so important that parents must know their kids. Not only know your kids' intellectual ability but know their pressure points. Parents need to know when kids hit the wall and want to run from an issue, rather than deal with it.

How do you know your kids? Simple answer. Talk to them. In the above IRL, it is best when the parent and kid can figure out what the problem may be together.

CHAPTER 9

POSITIVE
SELF-ESTEEM=OPTIMAL
ACADEMIC ACHIEVEMENT

C all me a broken record. I'll say it once again; we must focus on the entire *well-being* of a kid. Life is just not about getting to an Elite School. It's also about raising a kid that has a positive self-esteem and will be able to navigate challenges throughout their lifetime, not just in that 7th grade math class.

You can only strive to be 'the best you can be' when you have positive self-esteem and are emotionally happy.

Once again, can we talk? I am asking you to do the impossible. How in heaven's name can a parent determine whether their kid is happy and has a positive self-esteem?

Let's face it – some kids, particularly those moody, hormonal teenagers, may not reveal their inner most feelings to mom and dad #NOSURPRISE. Some kids, even if they are happy, do not speak in complete sentences to their parents #NOSUPRISE. At best, they grunt or mumble one syllable words. It is okay to laugh. You know what I am talking about! This is what we parents deal with day in and day out with kids in high school.

The easy answer is to just talk to your kids and ask them. The problem is that they may not be truthful or reveal their innermost feelings. In addition to talking to your kid, the best place to start is by attending parent-teacher conferences at school.

My husband and I have always talked with our kids. To this day, we have meaningful conversations with our sons about their work, social life, and current events. When they were in K-12, we knew what classes they were taking, how they were progressing, and how they felt about the class and the teacher(s). We met with their teachers, to not only confirm how our child was doing academically, but also to learn how he was engaging socially with his other classmates.

To clarify, this is not being up your kid's #ASS. Simply stated, we were always *in tune* with our kids. It was reasonable and appropriate for us to #RAISETHEBAR.

As a parent, why should you be concerned, or quite frankly, care if your child has an 85% in math? This is a *'it depends'* answer. If a parent knows their child on an emotional and academic level, then they may be able to assess what, if any, intellectual limitations their child has. If your child's goal is to attend a top university, grades lower than a 90% are just not acceptable. To many readers, this may sound harsh. Again, it is imperative that a parent really know their child to accurately assess what they truly #NEED.

It is very easy to send your kid to school every day. A parent can have the attitude that it is the school's responsibility to educate their child, and the child's responsibility to learn. Remember #DUMPANDRUN.

When my husband and I raised our children, we never had the pleasure of solely relying on the school to educate our kids. We always had very high (but reasonable) expectations that we felt were proportional to our kids' abilities. And yes, many educators and parents laughed at me and thought we were too hard on our kids.

It is a shame that some people, even educational professionals, do not understand what it feels like, on an emotional level, to a child when they underperform and fall well below their intellectual and academic potential.

Kids are not happy when they do not achieve their potential. Why should they settle for less? Would you?

THE MIDDLE SCHOOL YEARS ARE
THE FOUNDATION FOR FUTURE
ACADEMIC SUCCESS

College is not just *something* you apply to in your senior year in high school. I mean, you can, but I certainly do not recommend that plan. Clearly, when I raised my kids, it was my intent to prepare them for life and all its challenges.

In many ways, my perspective of getting kids ready for Schools differs from most people. As a parent, when my kids went to school, they were going to work. School was their full-time job. They were always expected to perform to the best of their abilities, every day.

Middle school is the time to begin to prepare kids for College. During the 'middle years', kids are older and should be able to comprehend the importance of an education and to take responsibility for their work product.

As parents, our goal is to always look forward to the future. This is a pivotal time to begin laying the foundation for future Elite School selections. It is in middle school that the foundation for high school is established. You might think I am putting the cart before the horse, but we must always be on the lookout for critical moments at which we can help secure our kid's future opportunities.

Here is an IRL example... Let us refer to the highly intelligent 8th grade student who is struggling in math. In this instance, we must look beyond a kid not doing well in math in just 8th grade. Consider what larger implications this may pose. The big picture is that in four years this same kid will apply to Colleges, and in eight years that same kid will, hopefully, be employed in the work force.

I know, you really think I am nuts for thinking this far ahead, but this is how I roll. Just stay with me...

The problem this student is experiencing in 8th grade math may just be a glitch, or could be symptomatic of a learning impairment, or, heaven forbid, this kid is simply not the mathematician we were praying for. But, wait a minute.

This 'glitch' may just be the reason this kid is not able to fulfill their academic potential and attend that Elite Schools in the future. Do you want to be the parent who did not intervene in 8th grade to fix that 'little' problem with math?

A parent must consider the totality of their kids' strengths and weaknesses. One of the most difficult times of parenting is when you must encourage (gently 'push') your smart middle schooler to *soldier on* through challenging academic classes. BTW, this is called dealing with 'Adversity'.

If you know your child has the aptitude and ability to excel in academics, then it is perfectly reasonable to have high expectations for your child to earn straight A's in all subjects, despite any learning difficulty they may encounter during middle school and high school. As a parent, you must be keenly aware when issues arise.

Keep in mind that you must be very supportive when you guide your child through these potentially difficult learning periods. In addition to providing parental emotional support and love, you may have to address learning impairments outside of school. This will require you, as the parent, to hire tutors to supplement your child's learning. In this regard, an educational learning specialist may be required to address specific learning deficiencies.

Therapists should also be added to this learning team. Therapists are 'shining stars', because they can help you understand the psychological make-up of your child and can also provide invaluable parenting guidance. At some point in this journey, you may want to consult with an educational therapist, who can administer I.Q. tests, to determine your child's I.Q. and the presence of any learning or developmental impairments.

WHEN YOUR KID SAYS THANK YOU

I can only speak from experience, but *when* (not if!) your child overcomes their learning impairment and succeeds in the class that was dragging them down not only emotionally, but lowering their overall GPA, they will *thank you*. You will get that *thank you* hug because you did not let them run away from the problem. They will *thank you* because you recognized there was an issue, got them that tutor, and you did not let them fail that class. They will *thank you* because you removed the back door to escape (run away) – which is the option to drop to an easier class. They will *thank you* because you ripped up those essays. Yes, they knew those drafts were garbage, but were too lazy to write them correctly the first time. They will *thank you* because they recognized the hours upon hours you spent teaching them to write, not only improved their writing skills, but reinforced the importance of a regimented work ethic.

Perhaps someday *your* kids will say *thank you* to you, because you helped them become the adults they are today.

When I talked to my friends about this book, we discussed the correlation between a kids' academic performance and their self-worth. Everyone agrees that somewhere in their kids' academic K-12 experiences, there was a major bump in the road that derailed learning and achievement. Furthermore, many friends agreed that the issue was never fully resolved.

Upon reflection, each of my parent-friends agreed that this occurrence marked the beginning of the end for achievement in one or more courses. Their kids' self-esteem went down the tubes, and most noticeable was how their son or daughter did not perceive themselves as 'smart,' 'capable,' or worthy of being 'Elite College material.'

What becomes of these kids in the 21st century? What place will they assume in the work force, in society, and in your family?

Here is another IRL that exemplifies what could have *been* if adults did not intervene...

When "Peter" was in 10th grade, I asked him which Schools he was thinking about attending. At that time, he was a very competitive athlete. The sport was suddenly derailed due to an injury. At age 15, Peter had to put all his efforts back into the classroom. Just a small problem – he did not perceive himself as a 'student.' At that age, if you are not a student, then what are you? It was pity that he had a self-image low enough to consider himself 'not smart,' due to learning impairments that had plagued him throughout his life. I was saddened by this and made it a point to, over the next several months, to motivate him to see himself in a better, positive light. I spoke with his parents and shared our discussion. Then, we all worked together to get this wonderful boy on a path to be a student, who was motivated to learn.

Fast-forward five years. "Peter" is currently thriving in College and looking forward to a future career in business. #KUDOS to him! College has become the platform for him to mature into a man and to learn that he can compete with his peers on an intellectual and professional level.

REMEMBER: … *Any* mind is a terrible thing to waste.

CHAPTER 10

THE HAPPY FACTOR

We must take a moment to address the happy factor, which is indicative of a state of mind. your kid. is indicative of a state of mind. The happy factor is the invisible happiness gauge that we all possess. and visible when we smile, heard when we laugh, or felt in a hug. The #HAPPYFACTOR, when present, enables us to #ACHIEVE.

For adolescents, I believe happiness occurs when they are socially and emotionally adjusted. Everyone needs these two elements in their lives, and these are crucial factors for adolescents.

In truth, when your kid is poised to apply to College, if your child lacks the #HAPPYFACTOR, as a parent, you should think twice to send him/her to any College or University, let alone an Elite one.

I cannot stress enough the importance of happiness. We know that *top grades* and *test scores* are required to be a Qualified applicant. However, happiness is reflected in a child who interacts well with peers, possesses a positive self-image and self-esteem of oneself.

As we all know, when we are not happy, we do not feel good about ourselves, and this can hinder our ability to perform, achieve and to simply function every day.

As kids progress from middle school to high school, and beyond, many parents of adolescents agree that not all kids are happy. This statement troubles all parents. And many of these parents do not know why. Why are kids depressed? Why are kids anxious? And, most alarmingly, why is the suicide rate amongst teens so high these days?

One answer is technology. Our kid's lives are influenced by the constant barrage of social media alerts they receive on the smart phones or computers. Our kids can never escape peer pressure. There is simply no relief, no emotional pause button, thanks in part to social media.

Think back to your own days in high school... the peer pressure to be accepted and fit in socially were present, but at least we tried to escape these feelings of insecurities when we were at home, which was our safe place. Kids today have nowhere to hide, because social media is everywhere. Kids are exposed to electronics at a young age. Electronics can be both a blessing and, conversely, extremely problematic. It is through the digital age, that our global society has become an actual click away. There is so much content, information, and connectivity to everything and everyone, that it has truly revolutionized the way we learn, educate, and socialize.

As a parent who has raised kids when smart phones were first becoming available, I immediately saw that this new technology was going to affect how kids would grow up. There is just something about that cell phone that draws kids to it like a magnet. This undeniable attraction starts when they are babies. When the kids are young, we encourage them to play video games and watch videos on our phones, all to allow us a few minutes of 'peace' from parenting.

The phone becomes a babysitter. We are all guilty of doing this from time to time. Sometimes, when you just want to have a few minutes to yourself, or have an adult conversation, it is just easier to hand the cell phone over to your nagging kid.

Parents forget that the smart phone is really a computer, and computers really require training to use. The problem with electronics is that our children are not educated in how to safely use their cell phone. As kids get older, most parents surrender to buying their kids their own phones.

However, parents do not supervise their kid's use of the phone. As a result, many kids play games, watch videos, and become addicted to social media. In this way, kids begin to seriously fritter away their precious time to learn.

An adolescent's unsupervised use of social media consumes most of their daily lives, and they are always plugged in. Most parents give their kids free reign to do what they want on multiple social media platforms. Yes, we do.

Kids monopolize their time texting friends, or studying photos posted by their peers on Instagram and Facebook. Peer pressure is hard enough when confined to face-to-face interactions. Now, as social media weaves it through every waking minute of our children's lives, peer pressure's insidious power only grows and presents new challenges that are difficult to navigate. Coping skills are tested.

Adolescents are continually developing emotionally. During years, they can have a fragile self-esteem, because they are focused on their own self-image in their perpetual quest to be accepted by their peers. Social media can accentuate peer pressure because everyone only posts photos of personal experiences when they are happy, looking their best and beautiful. Everyone is seemingly #BLESSED.

When kids act as voyeurs, peeping in on the carefully curated Instagram feeds of their peers, they only see the good, not the bad and certainly not the ugly. It can be especially difficult for the emotionally developing adolescent to understand that these are just photos, and do not paint an accurate picture of what someone's life may be like. The lives of others are not perfect, even though it can appear so in photos. Adults have a hard-enough time understanding and remembering that.

Imagine the burden we place on children when we expect them to navigate this same difficult terrain on their own.

It is our obligation as parents to teach our children to use these devices responsibly.

We willingly buy our kids these phones, many of which cost an absurd amount, and then we pay a monthly usage charge on top of that. Oh yes, we pay dearly for our kids to use their phones. Our kids can't afford these phones. I hate to say this, but when you think about it, parents are weaponizing their kids with electronic devices. In truth, most kids are not mature enough to appreciate the #POWER of the smart phone.

Science has my back on this idea, too. A human brain is not fully developed until age 25. Yes, age twenty-give. Therefore, we must be cognizant of the fact that adolescents are impulsive and have not acquired the proper skill set to filter their thoughts and actions and behave in a manner that lays the groundwork for future success in society. That is why kids often run into so much trouble when using smart phones...It is not that they do not know how to use a smart phone, but kids have not yet learned how to use a smart phone safely.

We expect our children to attend school, thrive and soar academically. Yet, they are now overloaded with Facebook, Instagram, Twitter, etc. These platforms give them license to express their thoughts instantaneously, unfiltered, and unsupervised. The playground is no longer limited to the schoolyard. It now encompasses the whole world, and this means the social pressures imposed on our children are #PROFOUND.

It is imperative that all parents understand that they must be a strong presence in their children's lives. It is our responsibility to guide and teach them. Goal setting is crucial now. In the 21st century, there is a higher incidence of depression, drug use and suicide of adolescence at a young age. We as parents must first and foremost be aware of and safeguard the emotional wellbeing of our children.

#WISEWORDS: Our child's #HAPPYFACTOR is crucial for a healthy physical development of their mind, body, and spirit (for the holistic, health conscious parent).

CHAPTER 11

STARTING HIGH SCHOOL

T owards the end of 8th grade, parents are typically invited to attend a 9th grade Welcome to High School orientation. For those families that have 'thought about' their child attending an Elite School, the time has come to implement your strategy to attain that goal. Yes, this is the moment we have all been waiting for... roll up your sleeves and kindly pay attention!

At orientation, high school counselors will typically welcome you all to high school. "This is so incredibly exciting!" Not really, but I am trying to get everyone psyched for what lies ahead, so please indulge me...The race for the coveted Schools acceptance to an Elite Schools has officially begun!

To ensure that the incoming students will pay attention, high schools often host this annual event for parents and students to attend. Parents, here's your cue: elbow your kids throughout the meeting to pay attention.

REMEMBER: These students are still in 8th grade and are all about 13 or 14 years old. They are still babies! The transformation our kids undergo from 9th grade to high school graduation day is remarkable. They really do grow up, physically and emotionally. And as for us parents, sadly, we just get older, grayer, fatter and more forgetful.

But that's all for later. Now, we are sitting with our kids at the orientation, and the guidance counselors are talking about what to expect in high school. We are provided a curriculum booklet that contains a description of the classes offered for each academic year. We are also handed a sample transcript of a high school graduate.

The transcript is a record of the classes a student took each high school year, which includes the final grade they received, and their GPA. What the counselors do not say, is that the transcript tells the *academic story* of a high school student.

In fact, most parents and students do not realize the official transcript is the first and perhaps most important document the Admissions Officer will review in the application.

When you fast forward three years to when your kid is a high school senior, if the grades on that transcript do not meet a prospective Elite School's requirements for admission, the student will be #REJECTED. Period. End of discussion.

When this student begins their first year of high school, they are now formally building upon the foundation that we as overbearing parents so carefully sculpted throughout their academic childhood.

In middle school, the curriculum progressively gets harder, and students are typically given the option to take honors or non-honors classes. If your student is on an honors academic track, the natural progression would be to migrate to advanced placement AP courses when they start high school. AP classes are considered Schools level courses.

All AP exams are regulated by the good folks at The Schools Board, who are also responsible for the dreaded the Standardized Aptitude Test, fondly known by many as the SAT. We will be discussing AP classes and standardized tests to a more in-depth degree later in the book.

My point in mentioning AP classes now, is that it is important for the high achieving 8th grade student to situate themselves on the #HONORSTRACK. If their goal is to attend an Elite School, then students *must* transition to high school as an honor student.

It is my expectation that the same parent who has met with the middle school guidance counselor and attended parent teacher conferences, will continue to be vigilant as their kid enters high school.

◆ ◆ ◆

HOLD UP...
From this moment on in the book, my fellow brethren, you will learn in-

depth, the requirements to be a Qualified applicant to an Elite School. There-after, we will discuss *ad nauseum, yes, over and over,* how Admissions deter-mines whether the Qualified Applicant is Compelling.

Just a warning my fellow brethren. I have a bad habit of repeating myself, particularly when the subject matter resonates with me. My kids hate when I do this, and I am sure you will get tired of this as well. Just deal with it. Think of coping skills.

REMEMBER: It is the Qualified Compelling Applicant that is deemed *Eligible* by The Dean to be a contender for that golden admission ticket.

CHAPTER 12

HOW TO TRANSFORM A HIGH SCHOOL FRESHMAN INTO A QUALIFIED AND COMPELLING APPLICANT

W hen your kid is a High School senior and their game plan is to apply and get accepted to Elite Institutions, what must they be?

Repeat after me, a #QUALIFIED #COMPELLING applicant.

My fellow parents, the time has arrived for you to embrace the rules of engagement for applying a kid to an Elite Institution. It is your choice to heed these words of wisdom.

Thus, what are the requirements to be a *legitimate* applicant to an Elite College and/or University?

A Qualified and Compelling Applicant meets
or exceeds the following requirements
for Admission to an Elite School:

1. A transcript that confirms required honors and college level courses either completed or in progress;

2. Perfect to near perfect grades and standardized test scores;

3. Stellar EC's that portrays an #ENGAGED applicant.

4. All these qualities contribute to an applicant to be considered #COMPELLING.

As we all know by now, your high school senior will get #REJECTED from an

Elite School if he or she does not satisfy the requirements set forth by the Dean.

My dear brethren, get used to hearing the word #REJECTED.

Thus, is it a waste of time and money to apply to an Elite School if you are not a Qualified applicant? Hell yes. However, honey, it is your kid's choice. Please be prepared for #REJECTION. Oh shit! I used that word again!

Listen...it may not be the place for this yenta to tell any kid who is unqualified, they should not apply to their dream Schools.

Personally, I would rather spend money on a pair of shoes than piss money away on an application to a school that I know my kid will get #REJECTED from (My apologies for repeating this word). #NOBRAINER.

It is up to the applicant and their parents to review each College's #REQUIRE-MENTS for admission to determine whether they are a Qualified applicant to that specific Elite School. Parents and students all need to remove their rose-colored glasses or stop sniffing glue and embrace the selectivity College's require of Elite applicants.

The standard for admission to Elite Schools is high! In addition to grades and test scores, the Dean expect candidates to be accomplished outside of school. Sometimes it seems like Elite Schools are exclusively looking for young #VI-SIONARIES who will be the #LEADERS of our tomorrow.

Admissions considers both tangible and intangible qualities when evaluating a candidate.

◆ ◆ ◆

HOLD UP...

From this moment forward, everything that your kid has done as a high school student will be woven, one way or another, into their #PERSONAL-STORY. This story defines everything about them as an applicant.

Make no mistakes... Elite Schools typically require applicants to take the most challenging courses their high school offers, and the Dean expects to see a transcript that reflects straight A's.

#FUTUREPLANNING: This is when we often hear the phrase, "I wish I knew then what I know now." Imagine if you could go back in time to when you still had the power to guide your kid through middle school.

Do you remember when your kid was in 8th grade and attended the high school orientation? If the plan then was for your kid to attend an Elite School, just think how helpful it would have been to start high school with an academic and extra-curricular game plan that reflected the admission requirements.

#WISEWORDS: When you attend the high school orientation, drag your kid to meet their future guidance counselor. Take it a step further, and schedule a meeting between you, your child, and the guidance counselor to discuss the course schedule for the freshman year of high school.

As the name might hint, the guidance counselor is the most important person to #GUIDE your child throughout high school. In fact, a proficient counselor could be the most influential person to help your child throughout the Schools application process.

Applying to an Elite School is truly a team effort, and successful applications are due to the collective effort of not only of the student, but also of the team that you the parent assembles to shape that student into a proper applicant.

Guidance counselors are adept at strategizing a four-year plan for high school, replete with the requisite honors or non-honors classes that are not only necessary to graduate high school, but also to have a transcript that will fulfill the application requirements set forth by Elite Schools.

As a child begins high school, a parent should continue their involvement with their child on every level – academic and emotional.

Participate in the planning of your child's high school academic roadmap. Meet with their high school guidance counselor and learn the expectations of the school and the courses that are available. As you guide your child throughout high school, it is critical for your parent-child relationship to be strong.

I am not saying that a parent should be 'best friends' with their kid, but based on my own parenting experience, a close relationship with your son or daughter can be mutually fulfilling during these stressful, hormonal years between a developing adolescent and perimenopausal mom. You want open lines of communication, which is a result of hard work and not prayers.

Throughout my life, I have found that in truth, many people are lazy. It is amazingly easy to be unmotivated to do anything. Everyone needs to be pushed to do something at one point or other in their life.

Some kids are self-motivated and eager to do their homework every night and study for exams or practice for a big tennis tournament. But many kids really need a #TUSH-PUSH to get them motivated. I mean let's be serious for a moment, have you ever seen a 14 or 15-year-old kid come home from school eager to sit down at their desk and study?

Based on my own personal experiences as a M-O-M, I learned that it is through maturation, goal setting, a structured home environment, and defined expectations that a child becomes #RESPONSIBLE for their own actions and destiny. Come to think about it, that is how I became a better parent and grew up too. Go figure.

◆ ◆ ◆

Moving on...

REMEMBER: My motto... Why be ordinary when you can be extraordinary? Kids are happiest when they achieve to their #FULLESTPOTENTIAL. Regardless of what the goal may be, they know that they accomplished all of which they are capable.

When you truly know what your kids can do, you can teach them to strive to reach their potential. Work with your child and utilize the resources available to you in your kid's school and community.

REMEMBER: Guidance counselors are professionally trained to evaluate students. The counselors are adept at assessing those students who are high-achievers and can challenge them on an intellectual level. When the guidance counselor initially meets an incoming 9th grader, they take pride in the fact that they will be working with these young students for the next four years of high school. The counselor embraces each student as they progress through high school to ensure that students can accomplish their academic goals.

This is a two-way street. Of course, this only works if you and your child seeks out the guidance counselor. And that I will have to leave up to you and your kid...

#NOBRAINER.

CHAPTER 13

HOW TO DETERMINE IF YOUR STUDENT IS A QUALIFIED APPLICANT

I n the spring of your student's sophomore year of high school (a.k.a. 10th grade), it is time to begin the #OFFICIALSEARCH for Colleges. This is also when you will begin to schedule campus tours.

I know, you think this is #TOOSOON. I have made it crystal clear that the key to applying to Elite Schools lies in the academic, intellectual, and emotional preparation of a student.

It is for this very reason that, as a parent, you can never be too early to start your student's preparation to apply to an Elite Schools. Okay, 8th grade could be a bit too early to physically tour College Campuses, but 10th grade is perfect timing. Why? Believe it or not, when your kid is in 10th grade, your kid will be graduating from high school in two years, and in less than 1.5 years he or she will be applying to Colleges.

The *impact* on us parents: #TIMEFLIES #ANOTHERGREYHAIR #4MOREWRIN-KLES #BOTOX.

BE REALISTIC WHEN RESEARCHING SCHOOLS, NOT IDEALISTIC

When you begin to research Colleges, you must be #REALISTIC while evaluating the Qualifications of your student. The first step is to determine whether your kid will be a *Qualified* applicant when they apply to Schools in the fall of their senior year.

As we have discussed ad nauseum, you and your kid should know by the Spring of 10th grade whether they are on a path to meeting the admission requirements. It is important to determine this status because you do not want to #WASTE your time, money and efforts touring schools when your kid does not meet the requirements for admissions.

REMEMBER: If they do not meet the requirements, they will be #REJECTED when they apply in 1.5 years.

#REALITYCHECK: Rejection is not easy, and this process can be a nightmare for most adolescents and, of course, parents.

If your 9th or 10th grade kid *realistically* wants to attend an Elite School, then it is up to YOU, the parent, to pace this race. It is easy to liken this quest to running a #MARATHON. This is a long, calculated process, in which your child must maneuver high school classes and EC's to enable him or her to be at a minimum, a Qualified applicant.

As your kid progresses through high school, this dream becomes harder to attain due to the increase in advanced classes and the growing expectation to achieve academic excellence.

THE DEAN REQUIRES APPLICANTS TO TAKE THE HARDEST HIGH SCHOOL CLASSES

For the intelligent, high achieving student, their 10th grade academic schedule must be packed with honors and AP classes. 10th grade is the year in high school that foreshadows the final transcript of a graduating high school senior.

To drill it into your head, academic achievement in 10th grade creates the foundation to make future College decisions. The ability to take honors classes in high school is predicated on the academic success of the previous school year. Many high schools offer honors classes as 'invitation only', based on academic achievement in a prerequisite course.

A Qualified applicant is a high school senior, who has fulfilled all required honors and AP courses required by the Elite Schools. Hence the reason it is crucial to know what to expect *in advance* of applying to an Elite School.

REMEMBER: The Dean wants an applicant to take the most challenging academic courses offered at their high school.

UTILIZE COLLEGE REFERENCE GUIDES

The best tool to use when you begin your Schools quest is a reference guide that lists all U.S. Universities and Colleges. Here is an easy task… Go to the library, or better yet, go to Amazon and buy a book. A comprehensive guide lists the Colleges and Universities and specific information as it pertains to each one. This is a wonderful tool that gives you a snapshot of the Colleges.

Researching Schools is easy. Astonishing! There is something easy in this whole crazy process! The first thing that you learn when you get your hands on a College Research Guide is that there are so many Universities and Colleges throughout the United States. I am confident that you will first research Elite Schools. This is just what kids and their parents do. You are aiming for the stars. #BEENTHEREDONEIT.

Regardless of which type of school you focus on, reference guides are helpful because they supply summaries of about every College and University in the United States.

The guide identifies each school's specific requirements for admission such as the statistics of the previous year accepted first-year class size, the number of men and women accepted, and the diversity of the class, specifically ethnicities, religions, and cultural backgrounds. You will learn where the school is located, namely if it is in an urban or rural setting, the cost of annual tuition, room and board fees, and percentages of scholarship recipients.

Now is the time to get out a yellow pen to start highlighting or get a few 'stickies' to tab pages for future reference #FUNFACT.

A quick way to determine whether your student is a proper applicant for a specific School at first glance is to go by the numbers. All Universities and Colleges will all identify a range of GPA, SAT, ACT, and AP scores the *current accepted first-year class* achieved. This range is important because it classifies your student and allows them to determine whether they have met the same threshold and should therefore apply.

The days of the 'Hail Mary's' of acceptances are over – there are just too many applications to Elite Schools. To even *think* that admissions will accept your kid 'just because' is foolish. Many parents and applicants secretly hope that admissions will *'mistakenly'* accept them. I have news for you – this ain't gonna happen!

◆ ◆ ◆

MOVING ON...

If your kid is in the ballpark of the Elite School's grade and score requirements, then you can learn more about the school. And just a reminder... satisfying these requirements does not guarantee an acceptance. It just means that if your child does apply for admission, they may, yes just 'may,' make it past the First Round of the admissions process.

WHAT IS A SOFT APPLICANT?

Later in this book we will discuss the additional requirements Elite Schools may consider in the event your student is at the lower end of the admissions' range. If the applicant has a Unique attribute or skill set that piques admissions' interest, but the standardized test scores or GPA is at the low end of the admissions' requirements, your kid may be viewed as a #SOFTAPPLICANT.

Between you and me, this means your kid is a borderline applicant and is straddling the proverbial fence, which is not optimal. Although beggars can't be choosey, and we'll take whatever crumb the Dean throws our way!

There is good news for a Soft Applicant. Some Elite Schools will conduct a #HOLISTIC REVIEW of the application. Thank you, Dean! This is where the applicant has some Unique, Extraordinary attribute, that may overshadow a weakness in one part of the application.

Do not be fooled by the term 'holistic' and lulled into a false sense of security. A Holistic Review is not where the admission office lights lavender scented candles and sits in a circle, holding hands to review the soft applicant's file.

Quite the contrary. A holistic review keeps the application out of the reject pile. If you have a borderline student and admissions holistically reviews their application, get on your knees and shout hallelujah for this #OPPOR-TUNITY!

#FUTUREPLANNING is a means to an end. When parents know their student is applying to a 'reach' school, the application must showcase the Unique qualities of the student and how he or she will #CONTRIBUTE to the first-year class and school community.

This is another reason why the end of 10th grade is an appropriate time to evaluate your kid's credentials as an applicant. The credentials are the tangibles – the GPA, final grades in each subject, a few AP test scores, and a PSAT, SAT, and/or ACT official test score.

I know what you are thinking – too soon? No, it is not too soon. In fact, this is perfect timing! Your kid should be on track with an honors curriculum for the remainder of high school in anticipation of applying to Elite Schools.

Hopefully 10th grade will be finished on a year-end high, with straight A's in all subjects. Honey, this was will be a warmup for the year from hell, 11th grade.

THE OPTIMAL RANGES FOR
STANDARDIZED TEST SCORES

This is also the time we start to talk about Standardized Tests. My favorite part of applying to an Elite School is when we needlessly 'torture' our kids to take these obnoxious exams. Just kidding, not funny.

Perhaps I am a bit 'severe' in my characterization of these exams, after all, they are a means to an end. I personally loathe these exams because they require so much preparation that eats through the time of an already packed schedule. Standardized tests also add a tremendous amount of pressure to kids who are already *stressed* out.

Tenth graders take a practice SAT, known as the "PSAT," and may have already received their scores by the time you tour Colleges in the spring. Elite Schools require high standardized test scores that are well above the national average for admissions. The ACT range is from 31 (low end) to a 36 (perfect score). Similarly, the SAT range is a 1400 (low end) to a 1600 (perfect score). AP test scores should be either a 4 or a 5, and the SAT Subject Test scores should range from 700 to 800.

Realistically, Elite Schools prefer #PERFECT SAT, ACT, AP, and SAT Subject Test Scores. Of course, they do, because they can.

Not surprisingly, *many* applicants to Elite Schools boast perfect scores, which is nothing short of amazing.

As a parent, you marvel at the kids that achieve a perfect score. That is an accomplishment. How do they do it? Oh, and by the way, I am referring to the kids that really get that high score, not #VARSITYBLUES.

But what can we parents do to help our stressed-out kids? We must work within the system and *support* our kids during this physically and emotionally draining time.

Here are a few IRL examples of just how kids deal with stress immediately prior to taking the SAT or ACT. When you drive your kid to take the SAT/ACT on a Saturday morning at 7:00am, do not talk in the car, do not offer advice and just smile. When your kid is so stressed out and needs to puke on the way to the test, pull the car to the side of the road and just wait. Let's not forget the kid who cannot leave the house, because they are so nervous, they can't get out of the bathroom. Yes, these are the kids who have studied for the standardized tests for over a year, day in and day out, and understand the importance of getting that high score.

Our kids suffer throughout the preparation for and taking of these tests. They deal with the agony, pain, and of course, the defeat of getting a low score. Most of our kids will take these tests multiple times, bouncing between the SAT and ACT, in the quest for the holy grail of a high score.

Not fair, not right that Varsity Blues Parents allegedly bribed proctors and other testing officials to alter low test scores. Perhaps this is another reason why so many parents were furious when they learned of the Varsity Blues Scam. We will *not* become those *desperate parents* who bought off proctors to change our kids' test scores.

REMEMBER: It takes a lot more than grades and test scores to get you accepted to an Elite School.

◆ ◆ ◆

The Dean Determines: Which Applicant is The Right "Fit" For Their Elite Institution!

In the frenzied application process, it is fair to say that most parents do not catch their breath to determine whether the school is a #GOODFIT for their kid. I got news for my fellow parents... you or your kid may not think about this, but this is a key factor in the acceptance equation #FUNFACT.

The Dean considers each applicant within the context of whether the student is a 'fit' to their Schools and how they will contribute to the entering first-year class. Some Colleges are more STEM ("Science, Technology, Engineering, Math") focused, while others are more based in the liberal arts. Universities can be a mixture of both academic disciplines.

#WISEWORDS: Be careful what you wish for. Some students are so focused on applying to an Elite School solely to impress their peers that they overlook whether the College and/or University they are pining for is the *right fit* for them to learn and grow over the next 4 years.

It is true that kids and parents really do get caught up in the name game of applying to Schools, which again is no surprise. If your kid attends an elite private or public high school, as we previously discussed, there is a not-so-subtle pressure for kids to aspire to attend Elite Institutions. For many people in this situation, it is a 'logical' next academic step to go from one elite academic institution to the next. Let's face it – most of these students have worked incredibly hard throughout their young lives.

Many of these kids were led to believe that they would apply to an Elite School and get accepted merely because they had the grades, test scores, and an impressive list of ECs'.

OMG. Yes, I just stated that there is an expectation, or at least a belief held by many parents and kids, that if they attend the 'right' elite high school they will be able to 'sidestep' their way to an Elite School.

The problem is that tens of thousands of super intelligent over achievers all aspire to get accepted to the same College and/or University. Add into this mix the tens of thousands of students that do not meet the minimal requirements and still apply to these Elite Schools as their 'reach school'.

When all of these students apply to the same Elite Schools, what happens to the admission process? We get what we have now, which is more than 40,000 applicants for a first-year class that only has 1000-1500 spots! Hmmm... Do you get the picture? This is not an easy process!

Just to overwhelm you a bit more, it is fair to say that over the last five years the top 25 Colleges and Universities in the country have all tightened their requirements for admission.

Schools that were once considered a 'safety school' (a.k.a. not your 1st choice) are no longer a slam dunk. Some public Universities now have more than 130,000 applicants!

Did you ever wonder why the application process to Elite Schools is so competitive? What ever happened in the last few years to create this Schools hysteria? Easy answer.

Repeat after me. The Common App.

THE COMMON APP

Hello, meet the Common App.

This is the required document that is the #FIRSTCOMPONENT of a formal College application. The Common App is the repository for all the salient facts about an applicant, pedigree questions such as name address, family members, school, grades, official transcript, teacher recommendations, extracurricular activities, and all that other jazz that proves your kid has what it takes to get into said Schools or university. The Common App will be further described in Chapter 22.

STRATEGY

As a mom, I can say with confidence that I have seen many high school students focus on applying to Schools that are either a *reach* school, or simply the *wrong* school. Put in plain English... they do not belong at that school for a variety of reasons.

REMEMBER: Parents and students should research Schools that are *realistically* within reach.

As you may have started to understand, applying to an Elite Schools not only requires that the student possess superior qualifications, but it also takes a tremendous effort to formulate a strategy on the part of students and parents to attempt to secure an acceptance to their dream school.

Moreover, your kid's dream school may always end up as just that, a #DREAM. The rejection then becomes the #NIGHTMARE.

CHAPTER 14

PLANNING YOUR COLLEGE OR UNIVERSITY CAMPUS VISIT

T he best time to start this journey is during the spring break of 10th grade. If you normally take a family trip to relax, forget about it. Instead, plan a vacation where you can visit a Schools. Gee, what a fun filled, family bonding, road trip. Yes, much better to tour Schools than go on a vacation and chill out by the pool, soaking up rays while casually sipping a margarita.

This is precisely what we did when our eldest son was in 10th grade. No, we did not relax by a pool and sip margaritas. We travelled to Los Angeles and planned a few Schools campus tours. Thereafter we returned to the east coast to visit a few more Schools, where I froze my tush off.

Once you decide which Schools or Schools you want to see, I encourage you to schedule all tours at least one month in advance. You cannot just show up at a Schools and say, "We are here!" and catch a tour. The Office of Undergraduate Admissions will offer Informational (Info) Sessions and Campus Tours. High School spring break vacation is peak season for campus tours and sell out fast. Yes, limited spots available even for the campus tours.

ONCE YOU GET THERE...

Most Schools offer two tours, an informational session, and a tour of the campus. The Information (Info) Session lasts about one hour and can accommodate groups upwards of 60 people at a time. An admissions officer will meet with the group and introduce you to their school and give an overview of the admission requirements.

Your student will be informed of application requirements such as GPA, standardized test scores, AP or IB classes, class rank, EC's, Schools essay, deadlines for application, financial aid, and first-year class size. The admissions officer will field a variety of questions upon conclusion of the info session.

The most frequently asked question at the tours are "How many students applied to the most recent first-year class, how many applicants were accepted early decision, deferred, regular decision, wait-listed, and rejected?" These are always important questions because a prospective applicant needs to know how many 'spots' (a.k.a. seats) are available in the incoming first-year class.

When the info session is over, off you go to the Campus Tour. The tour is the fun and flirty part of all this because it is always led by a student who happily talks up the Schools, telling you why it is the greatest place on Earth. This part of the tour is important, not as much for its informational content (although the guides do know a host of campus facts), but because it gives your student an opportunity to better understand the #VIBE, or atmosphere, of the School.

I enjoyed the student led tours, not necessarily for the oohs and aahs of the campus, but because it was entertaining to watch the eager parents and candidates cozy up to the tour guide.

In fact, while touring an Ivy, I was astonished to see just how many hopefuls were drawn to their guides, all asking them pointless questions. It was as if the candidates thought these guides were the proverbial 'in' to the school and would somehow remember them and flag them for admissions. #WASTEOF-TIME.

Student tour guides, while great resources as to the quality of student life on campus, have #NOINFLUENCE over admissions. I am confident that none of those kids who questioned their guides to death were accepted to the Schools #SADBUTTRUE.

Campus tours provide the perfect forum for parents to experience all the conflicting emotions that surround the Schools process—fear, sadness, joy, and excitement all take hold while walking across the collegiate quad.

Some parents hold Kleenex, blowing their nose and dabbing their eyes, because they are sad that their little prince or princess is leaving the castle. Others smile in wonder at the opportunity they wish they had for themselves. I can assure you; I did neither. LIES! Let's not forget that I am Mommy.

If I recall, the first campus tour is a shocker. In truth, when you are looking at your kid on that first tour, it is sincerely hard to fathom just how fast #TIME-FLIES.

◆ ◆ ◆

MOVING ON...

Enough with the tearing up that your baby will be leaving home, which is not happening anytime soon. I snapped out of my nostalgic trance, and realized my son was in 10th grade and would be home for 2 more years. He was going nowhere fast. There was no time for tears. I had a weak, emotional moment, and it passed like *gas*.

I was on a mission. I sized up the competition – all brilliant-looking kids from prestigious private schools were in our tour group—I could not help but glance over at *my* son and shake my head in dismay. OY VEY! At the time of our Campus tour, despite having flawless grades, my kid would stand on the fringe of the group, slouched over. He was wearing jeans, sneakers and refused to play the part of the over-zealous, over-accomplished, brilliant College applicant.

My kids never wanted to follow along with the often-inauthentic role that all parents and counselors expected of them. No khaki pants and loafers for my boys! Their preferred uniform was ripped and faded jeans, a tee shirt emblazoned with a rock band logo, and converse sneakers (black, of course.).

Food for thought crazy parents: does it really matter how your kids dress on the tour? Should you be concerned if your kid is not wearing apparel you deem appropriate. Once again, you are not applying to the Schools, your kid will be the applicant. The brilliant, Extraordinary non-conformist needs to convey their *individualism* to the Dean.

Touring Elite Schools with a second semester high school sophomore is an eye-opening experience. The concept of attending College is slowly becoming a reality, and the admission tours are starting to overwhelm them. Perhaps standing shoulder to shoulder with their competition at these tours contributes to their anxiety, or listening to admissions list the onerous, staggering requirements is sending them down the rabbit hole. Yes, this fear does pass like *gas* once the tour begins.

And yes, beware of being in these small groups when walking throughout the campus and buildings. Kids and parent are so nervous, lots of *gas*.

Now, your kids can finally see for themselves what an Elite School looks like. What do our prospective Elite students want to see? Do they want to see the classrooms, lecture halls, or labs? Of course not! They want to see the dorm rooms, the gyms, and the dining halls! Some dorms are amazing– the millennial student has many needs, which we already know of because we created these needy children. These high-end dorms are now replete with Wi-Fi, wall to wall carpeting, air conditioning, exercise facilities, common rooms with ping pong and foosball tables, vending machines, large flat screen TVs, and a shared kitchen. Many Schools now feature restaurants that serve sushi, vegan food options, and other specialty cuisines instead of the slop they fed *us* in the dining halls of our day.

This is *not* the Colleges of Christmas' past, or the shit-hole dorms we lived in. That is for sure #REALITYCHECK of the good old days, when we had no choice. We had the choice between this shitty dorm or that shitty dorm, and the food that was disgusting. There were no food choices, the same slop was served at each dining hall. The cuisine changed from day to day but was always shitty. If I recall, a special sauce, called ketchup, could really add zest to any dish.

But not all Elite Schools ascribe to this modern glitz and glam. I have seen some dorms that are so old school that, in some ways, they turn off a prospective student from applying – even when the school is prestigious. Let's be honest, these kids have worked hard to get to a top Schools, and the last thing they would to do is 'rough it.' This generation knows how to live! And it appears that many Colleges are now in a race to #UPGRADE their respective campuses to fit the needs of the 21st century student.

Elite Institutions have the current technological bells and whistles, because they recognize that top-notch students want to study in an environment that motivates them to achieve. Our kids appreciate living and working in an environment that is cutting edge, and these Schools are continually enhancing and renovating their facilities to lure the smartest students... Not like the tens of thousands of prospective top candidates need one more reason to flood their school with applications.

#FUTUREPLANNING: The earlier you start researching Elite Institutions, the more realistic your child's expectations will be when they start to apply in their senior year. This also give your kid the reason they need to tush-push themselves just a little bit more to get great grades!

CHAPTER 15

THE ADVISORY TEAM: HIGH SCHOOL GUIDANCE AND COLLEGE COUNSELOR; PRIVATE COLLEGE ADVISOR; SAT/ACT/ COACH; COLLEGE ESSAY EDITOR

HIRE EVERYONE
(IF YOU CAN AFFORD IT)

Congratulations! You have arrived at the point where you decide if you want to hire a College advisor. Wait a minute... You are probably thinking, "This sounds like it is going to start costing me more money, on top of the money we are paying for tutors, school exams and standardized test prep!" And isn't the high school guidance counselor the College advisor? Why would you have to hire a private College advisor?

I have always maintained that when your child is high achieving and wants to apply to Elite Schools, it takes a #VILLAGE. When my kids applied to College, I called it the #TEAM.

What I learned during *my* team's journey, is that counselors, teachers, and advisors are more energized to help a *motivated* student apply to Schools when the parent is also onboard. Yes, I said energized! Get with the program...

Applying to Elite Schools can be a grueling process, so your mind set must be positive. Your job as the parent is to be the motivational speaker not only for your kid to be a superior student, but to get the other 'players' on your 'team' pumped up to help your kid.

REMEMBER... A parent only has one kid to focus on getting into College, while the other team leaders could have hundreds of kids they are simultaneously guiding through the process.

WHAT DOES A GUIDANCE COUNSELOR REALLY DO?

The high school guidance counselor is the orchestral leader of the high school curriculum and Elite application process. Yes, the guidance counselor may just be the most important person on your kid's team. Second only to the tiger mother who is, obviously, the leader of this universe.

Once again, if you and your child have already *established* a relationship with the guidance counselor early on, this person will be able to provide insight into potential College choices that will complement your student. I maintain that the guidance counselor is the most influential person who helps a student apply to Elite Schools.

When the tiger mom, guidance counselor, and student are working together from the very beginning of high school, the counselor will have time to design a *complete blueprint for a masterful transcript.*

A competent counselor is always looking forward, designing a rigorous academic schedule that will act as the foundation of their student's future beyond high school. Trust me, the guidance counselor understands the importance of a near perfect final transcript.

In fact, it is the high school guidance counselor who is the unsung hero. For some reason, most parents do not know this #FUNFACT. Guidance counselors not only *want* to *know* their students but *want* to help them navigate through any social or academic issues that arise during high school. The guidance counselors I have met like their jobs and enjoy working with students. Guidance counselors, like us parents, are rooting for their students to #SUCCEED.

Guidance counselors are keenly adept at integrating high school curriculum with Elite Schools admission requirements. In this regard, the counselor's wealth of knowledge is priceless.

When guidance counselors know that their entering freshman student is aspiring to attend an Elite School, the planning of academic schedules for each successive year of high school is critical to further that goal. It is a great idea for both you and your kid to meet with the guidance counselor at the beginning and end of each academic year.

If you think for one second that these bi-annual meetings portray you as an over-bearing parent, you are totally wrong. Guidance counselors want to work with academically engaged students, who have parents that encourage their intellectual and emotional development. In fact, counselors contact the student's current teachers in preparation for these meetings. This enables the counselor to provide an accurate assessment of the student's current academic progress in each class.

As you know by now, there is more to life than just grades and test scores. Teachers and guidance counselors do not just teach. They observe the totality of their student's wellbeing in an academic and social setting. Their observations of the student, your child, are important for a multitude of reasons. First and foremost, every parent should want to know whether their adolescent is socially adjusted among their peers and is HAPPY. See Chapter 10 #HAPPYFACTOR.

We all want our kids to soar academically. If they are not happy, their academics are bound to suffer. In today's world, many adolescents suffer from depression, anxiety, and stress. This must be addressed. It is so important that parents be able to gauge how their kids are doing.

The guidance counselor can act as a #CHECKPOINT when assessing your child's emotional wellbeing and, if necessary, suggest help.

Here is a news flash: It is common for teenagers to reveal their true personality to their teacher or guidance counselor. These are adult resources that are not their parents, so kids often feel more comfortable discussing their fears, hopes and failures honestly.

THE GUIDANCE COUNSELOR'S 'SECRET POWER'

Did you know that the counselor has access to the school's master academic schedule? Do you know how helpful this can be when your kid needs to change his or her schedule or request a different teacher? The guidance counselor can take care of these types of changes with a quick email or phone call to the teacher. If you do not have a relationship with your guidance counselor, your student can encounter many roadblocks when trying to adjust their schedule...

MELTDOWN! This happens because most students and parents are truly #UNAWARE as to how their respective high school administration functions.

Your kid typically receives his or her academic schedule a week or so before the first day of school, and it is common that students' schedules will need to be adjusted. High school administrators use a computer program to create students' schedules for the upcoming academic year based on the classes requested by each student.

It's funny how the computer program is not particularly sensitive to your kid's subjective needs when academic schedules are *randomly* created. The computer program may not know, and certainly does not care, that your son or daughter does not want to attend that AP Chemistry class at 7:00am with the 'hard teacher,' who 'grades down', and 'deflates grades.' This, my friends, is just one example of when the counselor-student relationship is crucial for future academic success.

In truth, many kids are 'slow on the draw' when it comes to changing their own schedules. They view it as a hassle, because they have more important things to do, such as look at pics on social media. Oh, please fellow parents, you are not surprised. Your kid takes one look at that 7:00am class and bitches and moans, in fact cries "I can't get up that early!". Do you see your kid calling their guidance counselor to change the schedule?

My brethren, Parents, this is not the time to drag your feet. Scheduling modifications must be #SWIFT. Schedule adjustments are done manually by the guidance counselor, and all changes are dependent on class size and how much 'wiggle room' the school allots for changes. Yes, all schedule changes are made on a first come first serve basis. As the saying goes, 'you snooze, you lose'. When schedules need to be changed, run, do not walk to the guidance counselor.

When a student requests a schedule change prior to the start of school, the counselor will attempt to pick the best teacher and class time for a required subject. There is a *but*... the student must be at the head of the pack to contact the counselor requesting a change.

Guidance counselors are far less likely to *accommodate* an 'emergency' email request from a student they have never met than they are to help a student with which they have already established a stronger relationship.

Kids are typically assigned the same guidance counselor throughout all four years of high school. This proves to be invaluable for the counselor's ability to independently monitor their student's progress each academic year. The guidance counselor evaluates the academic performance and knows what the student can achieve. If there is any doubt as to future class placement, the counselor and teacher can meet to assess the student's ability in a specific subject.

I have heard many parents complain that the counselors are not helpful, but I disagree. Yes, guidance counselors are responsible for their students. However, it is unrealistic to expect a #MEANINGFULCONNECTION to develop overnight.

Many disgruntled students and their parents only met with the counselor once or twice throughout their four years of high school. Thus, they had no relationship. Come on now, can we talk? Let's be serious that one or two meetings is not enough time to get to know anyone!

THE GUIDANCE COUNSELOR IS THE MVP
OF ELITE COLLEGE APPLICATIONS!

In addition to helping their students through high school, the guidance counselor also plays a crucial role throughout the College application process.

Once again, you ask why? Most parents, if not all, and students, do not know that the Common App requires the high school counselor to write a Letter of Recommendation on behalf of the applicant.

Unbeknownst to parents and kids, the letter of recommendation from the guidance counselor is more important than the teacher recommendations. #FUNFACT.

When the guidance counselor provides information to a College or University about a student, they can contextualize their evaluation of a student's efforts not only as it relates to that graduating class, but as it compares to the *entire* high school. The guidance counselor reviews the student's high school academic record, standardized test scores, and extracurricular activities.

Upon review of the totality of the student's academic and extracurricular record, the guidance counselor will be able to provide an analysis of the student's present abilities and, most importantly, #FUTURE collegiate performance.

The Dean values the guidance counselor's letter of recommendation, because it provides, to a reasonable degree of certainty, their professional opinion of the applicant's intellectual ability among their peers on a local and national level.

TEACHERS AND TEACHING STYLES

Teachers are also valued in this process. I consider teachers to be the backbone of a school because they implement the curriculum and cultivate the student's minds with the information they disseminate. The academic success of a school is the result of how well teachers teach. It is their teaching that will 'make' or 'break' students.

More than just teaching math or english, teachers can also become mentors outside the classroom. Teachers have the power to profoundly impact kids... for the rest of their lives.

We all know that teachers are people, and like people, not all teachers are alike. Teachers have varying teaching styles and different expectations that can and will #IMPACT how students learn. Some teachers take a lecture approach expecting their students to self-teach, learning the curriculum outside of the classroom, and be responsible for knowing the material by the next time the class meets. Other teachers will spoon feed the material to their students. This type of teacher can be a more forgiving grader than the former type because their goal is to create an environment that encourages the adolescent to learn, even if that means stepping outside of their comfort zone and risking failure.

There is no 'one way' that students learn best. Some students flourish in a rigorous academic learning environment where expectations for achievement are high. The grading scale in this kind of environment can be considered unforgiving, and sometimes it seems like the teacher demands perfection. Some students find this is incredibly motivating.

Other students find this incessant onslaught too much. It is plausible that a student who is taking all advanced honors courses, simply feels they need to have at least one class that acts as a proverbial 'breather.' This does not mean that the teacher will just wave a magic wand and give the student an "A." However, the teacher's standards for receiving an "A" may be lower. BTW, this is totally *cool*.

Fellow parents, ask yourself: which classroom environment is most suitable for your kid? We parents want our kids to learn from a teacher that will elicit personal academic achievement. We want our kids to thrive in each classroom.

REMEMBER: The guidance counselor can help arrange schedules to accommodate varying teaching styles to optimize a student's academic achievement.

REMEMBER: The official transcript will only evidence the course taken and the grade received... There is no *asterisk* next to an honors class noting that the course was taught by a #BALLBUSTING teacher. Admission officers do not give extra points for subjecting yourself to the harder teacher.

Personally, I do not advocate that students take the AP course taught by the 'perceived-to-be-easier' teacher. Hell No!

Why? I am a tiger mom. I prefer the teacher who challenges their students to achieve their #PERSONALBEST. Of course, I do.

In the real world, we are always expected to put forth our best, not just the bare minimum. In many cases, the #BALLBUSTING teacher sets high, but reasonable, expectations that allow smart students to #RISE to the occasion and learn more.

What an accomplishment for any kid to receive a top grade in a class by a teacher known as #THEPUNISHER! Talk about your kid feeling intellectually empowered because they challenged themselves and our proud of their personal accomplishment.

You know it's coming, the *but*...we do not want to overwhelm our kid either. As we discussed, when a kid is taking all advanced honors classes, the academic workload is demanding, and these kids are way too stressed. It really is ok if they have a teacher that grades with a softer touch.

Once again parents, when your kid is putting together a new academic schedule for the upcoming school year, find out the level of difficulty of the class and familiarize yourself with the teachers and their styles.

Learning should always be a positive experience, where there is a symbiotic relationship between the student and teacher. Your new best friend, the Guidance Counselor will happily share this priceless information with you.

WHAT GUIDANCE COUNSELORS DO AFTER YOU SUBMIT YOUR APPLICATION

No, guidance counselors do not twiddle their thumbs after a student's application is submitted. They are still prodding their students to stay on task and repeat the mantra, "You cannot let up on your grades!"

HOLD UP...

Did anyone know that an Admission Officer may #CONTACT a guidance counselor while a student's application is under review? Yes, this really happens. #FUNFACT.

And by the way – once that College application is submitted, the student is not permitted to contact admissions. That rule applies to us crazy parents too. Even our hired gun, the private Schools advisor is not allowed to contact Admissions.

The only person allowed to speak with College admissions when an application is under review is our favorite person, the guidance counselor. #FUNFACT.

Hey parents, I have another #FUNFACT to share with you that will add to your already high blood pressure. Sometimes an application is #BORDERLINE, meaning that the applicant may have outstanding EC's that reflect a passion that has the potential of becoming a future career, but they do not have the level of test scores or GPA required by the Elite admissions department.

When this happens, admissions contacts the guidance counselor and requests a copy of the mid-semester grades. This can ensure that the student's first semester of 12th grade is still meeting the admission's GPA requirements.

Keep in mind, the guidance counselor is not permitted to inform the student that the admissions department is contacting them, they are the person who will provide the College with this information. The counselor must provide the student's current grades immediately, and if any grade has gone down, a borderline student could be rejected. Once again, the Guidance counselor may have to 'explain away' this lower grade.

Many students are under the impression that once that application is submitted, they are finished with school and grades, and can sit back and #COAST for the rest of high school. #FAKENEWS!

In truth, all acceptances are #CONDITIONAL and can be revoked at the discretion of the Dean. There are out there about kids who took 'senioritis' too seriously and received low grades during their last semester of high school. These students were #HORRIFIED to learn that their acceptances were #RESCINDED by the Elite School of their dreams.

#WISEWORDS: It is for this reason that all guidance counselors advise their students at the beginning of the senior year not to let up on any grades, even after they are accepted to their choice school. All applicants to Elite College and/or Universities must heed this warning!

COLLEGE ADVISORS

In addition to the guidance department, all elite private schools (and many public schools) have a College Counseling and Career Department. This department provides Schools advisors who are on staff to individually advise students throughout the College application process.

Some parents choose to hire a private College advisor for extra hand holding and tush-pushing.

REMEMBER: Not all kids are enthusiastic and gung-ho to apply to College. They want to apply *but* have more important things to do like check out Instagram feeds, or text their friends, or watch Netflix. We are dealing with teenagers. Just wait till you, my fellow parent will be up their #ASS to get them to fill out the applications and write those required essays. This is akin to pushing a boulder uphill.

Students typically meet with their assigned high school College advisor in 10th grade. Believe it or not, this is perfect timing. The high achieving students already have a few Elite Schools on their radar, and some kids even have a specific top choice they are gunning for.

BTW, this is a #REALITY check. This is another reason why applying to Elite Colleges is competitive. Kids start targeting these Schools a few years prior to applying.

To repeat for the hundredth time, parents cannot be ignorant or claim ignorance of the College application process! If you do not know what qualities the Dean wants in applicants, you will be of no help to your kids when they apply.

Be grateful if your kid's high school has a College advisor on staff. However, do not rely solely on them to help your kid apply to College. If it is that important that your high achieving, highly intelligent child attend an Elite Institution, then you *must* be involved in this process. Everyone makes mistakes, and there can never be too many eyes when it comes to reviewing an application.

◆ ◆ ◆

Moving on...

Now, we are really getting close to applying to College. The crescendo is building! I get goose bumps just thinking about what lies ahead for you and your kid.

The GOOD NEWS for you is that by the end of this book, you should be prepared for the Elite College admission process. At a minimum, you should know what to expect.

It is at this point that the College Advisor assumes their role of easing kids into the College search process...And you are aware of how this process unfolds.

THE NAVIANCE ACCOUNT

All students create a Naviance account, which is an American College and career readiness software provider that partners with high schools and other K–12 institutions to provide students with Colleges planning and career assessment tools. This program is typically introduced to students by their College advisor in 10th grade.

Depending on the size of the school, some private and public high schools have a College Advisory Department. This can be a terrific resource for students because there are several College advisors on staff whose sole function is to work with each student to oversee the application process in its entirety.

The College Advisor meets extensively with the student and reviews similar information that would be used to apply to Colleges. Namely, the Advisor has access to the usual suspects of grades, transcript, standardized test scores, and a resume prepared by the student that identifies all EC's.

The Advisor will create a comprehensive list of Colleges that are commensurate to the student's academic qualifications, area of study, type of campus, etc. At this meeting, it is common for the student to give the Advisor their Top 10 List of Schools they want to apply to.

The advisor will scan that list in a tenth of a second, and immediately identify the Colleges and Universities that are #REACH or #SAFETY schools for the student.

A Reach Schools is a College or University that is a real stretch ('reach') for the student to get accepted, meaning that they either fall short of the College admission requirements; does not meet the minimum admission requirements; insufficient EC's; or the Schools is highly selective, and most Qualified applicants are a #LONGSHOT.

On the other hand, a Safety School is a College or University that is a *safe* to school for the student to apply to. The student is a Qualified applicant and has easily met the requisite requirements for acceptance. In theory, acceptance should be a 'slam dunk'. Although these days, the Safety School reject the *over*-Qualified applicant. Can you guess why? The Dean knows this over-Qualified applicant applied to this College to be safe, with no intention of ever attending. #FUNFACT.

The College advisor will determine, based on a calculated strategy, the Colleges a student should apply Early Decision ("ED"), Early Acceptance ("EA"), and Regular Decision. Later in this book, we will discuss what each of these terms mean in the context of applying to an Elite School.

PRIVATE COLLEGE ADVISORS

So, if the high school guidance counselor and advisor are so helpful, why would you hire a private College Advisor for your student's team? As a parent or mentor of a kid applying to an Elite School in the 21st century, you are completely dependent on the College advisor to help maneuver your kid through the application process. I oversaw everything… but I knew my limitations.

For most students and families, this process is just too complicated and, quite frankly, overwhelming. I like collaborating with a few different advisors at once because everyone helps each other by contributing 'something'. Hence, the #TEAM concept.

There are so many nuances throughout the application process! The student and parent can really learn from everyone that they work with. In the end, it all depends if it is within your budget.

When you want to hire a private College advisor, you must look at their credentials. The College advisor may have been a high school guidance counselor and chose to work privately rather than stay in a school. The advisor may also be a former College admission's officer, who also chose to work privately and advise prospective applicants.

In this regard, it is always interesting to get insight from someone who worked 'on the inside' of the admission's office. Former admissions officers have reviewed tens of thousands of applications to elite Schools and know how the admission process works at this level.

They know why certain students are accepted and some are rejected, despite having the same qualifications, which is priceless. These advisors also know what the transcript should look like, what standardized scores and grades are required, and how the essays should read. In many ways, hiring this private advisor can give you a more #REALISTIC approach to applying to an Elite School.

They will tell you the truth, even if your kid does not want to hear it. Specifically, that there is absolutely no chance in #HELL your kid will get accepted to a specific Elite School.

Despite years of hard work, pain, anguish, suffering, and tons of money spent, no kid wants to hear they are *not* Qualified for admission. BTW, no parent wants to hear this doom and gloom news.

Therefore, you the responsible parent, must, hire the Schools advisor, who will tell your kid the truth. Think of this person as the outside consultant, who re-affirms the #TRUTH about your child's qualifications and dispels the misconceptions surrounding what their chances of acceptance will be to a variety of Elite Schools.

So, what do you do when you do not like the truthful, accurate information this top-notch professional, experienced College advisor, former admissions counselor tells you? You still do what you know is right in your heart as a parent, with one caveat. You must listen very carefully to everything they tell you about the Elite School process... and then you proceed with your kid's application as if you are playing a game of chess. #GOFORIT!

CHAPTER 16

GETTING DOWN TO BUSINESS:

THE OFFICIAL START OF THE
RACE TO APPLY

Once your kid is in the spring semester of their junior year, the time has arrived to meet with the private College advisor and decide whether that person would be helpful to your team. Whether you hire a private College advisor or rely on the high school advisor, the Schools process has officially started. The clock is now #TICKING.

The College advisor will discuss the courses your child took in high school, the grades they received, and their standardized test score(s). By the end of the spring semester of junior year, your child should have taken at least one standardized test, either the ACT or SAT. If their score is high, then the advisor says, "Good job". In the world of Elite Schools, the score is never high enough.

For example, a perfect composite score on the ACT is a 36. A composite ACT score of 32 is considered exceptionally good, but if you are applying to an Elite Schools, a 34 is better. In this process, grades or scores could always be #HIGHER. This is the reality your child must accept going forward. "You did a fantastic job, but it is not good enough."

Sadly, the advisor's critique does not get any better. If your AP test scores are anything less than a perfect 5, well that also affects your chances of getting accepted to an elite Schools. The advisor proceeds to rip apart the SAT subject test scores too. One advisor had told you that anything over a score of 700 is great, but then this advisor says you can only apply with a perfect score of 800. You are dizzy, and your kid feels like they are an idiot. Please #BREATHE.

There is some good news for standardized tests. More Colleges and Universities are moving towards being #TESTOPTIONAL. This means the applicant is not required to submit standardized test scores. Before you celebrate, remember that as of today, this is still a requirement at most Elite Colleges and Universities. Best to study and sharpen your pencils while you still have time! Elite Schools will always use some form of standardized assessment to compare students on a #NATIONALLEVEL.

MOVING ON...

After that incredibly upbeat (not!) conversation of standardized test scores and AP scores, the advisor asks your kid what he or she did over the last two summers. I was happy to hear this question given that, at the time, my son had just been accepted to a prestigious summer program. I was thrilled we could check off a proverbial box. The advisor was pleased, although *not* impressed. Frankly, I was ready to #GIVEUP and #THROWUP.

Did I mention that the advisor initially asked my son if he ever went to Africa to drill wells for water, or if he was researching a new cancer gene to aid with the creation of a vaccine? I had a sudden terrifying flash of an image—scrawny 15-year-olds wearing lab coats and discussing potential cures in squeaky prepubescent voices. Turns out he was #JOKING #NOTFUNNY. But by this point, we did not know if we should laugh or cry.

◆ ◆ ◆

HOLD UP...

SNAP OUT OF IT! You Have Lost Touch with Reality!

Let's freeze the clock for a minute. You are sitting there with the hired gun, AKA the College advisor. He is going on and on about all the accolades your child must have to be a Qualified applicant.

I know what you are doing. You are sitting there, in the room with your kid and the College advisor, and you are melting into your chair. You are not sure if a #HOTFLASH is coming on, but it is certainly getting warmer in that room.

You are listening to the College advisor rattle off the laundry list of the things your kid should have accomplished by now, the courses that should have been taken, and the SAT/ACT/AP scores that should have been achieved, and you feel as though your kid is a loser. You feel like you are a loser too because you did not push your kid harder. It is ridiculous to feel this way, but we all do.

This is what this application process does to us! It ruins us! We absolutely #LOSESIGHT of how hard our kids have worked for so many years. We are told that despite their achievements (which are incredible) our kid is #NOTGOO-DENOUGH.

And I thought my mother had me jump through platinum hoops when I was a kid. The hoops kids are expected to soar through for Elite Schools are not just platinum, they are encrusted with diamonds and rubies. The news is going from bad, to worse, to #SUCKS.

◆ ◆ ◆

HOLD UP...

Ask yourself if your kid is socially adjusted and happy.

We have approached the moment in the Elite Schools application frenzy in which it is easy to lose touch with reality.

As a parent, you must step back and think if this process is worth it.

Most applicants do not meet the requisite criteria for admission to an Elite School. Someone on the team must be #REALISTIC as to which Colleges your kid is *Qualified* to apply.

THE SILVER LINING: HOLISTIC APPROACH

All this said, I am the hopeless, or hapless, #OPTIMISTIC. I never take 'no' for an answer. And just when I thought all hope was lost and there was no chance my kid could or should apply to an Elite School, the advisor said, "Some Colleges take a #HOLISTIC approach when reviewing an applicant." #OMG! What does that mean? Does my kid still have a chance to apply to an Elite School? Yes! Yes, and yes!

The #HOLISTIC Approach means that an Elite School will consider the #TOTALITY of the applicant and not summarily #REJECT them for something like lower test scores. The 'totality' considers the successes, failures, and passions that this kid has displayed throughout high school and their life for that matter.

But... here is the big BUT. Your kid must possess some out of this world, Extraordinary, Unique skill set that *compensates* for their lack of a traditional requirement, such as grades or a high standardized test score.

Just wait one minute. Talking about perfect grades and test scores, advanced honors and AP classes really just gets to be too much, even for me.

When any parent is entrenched in the College application process, sometimes you just daydream about having that conversation with the Dean, saying "... I really hate when trivial things like grades or standardized test scores get in the way of my kid getting accepted to Elite Schools. Can't you just accept him because he is such a nice boy and tries hard?". That will never happen. But can't a mom just have that wishful thought? Duh, the answer is NO. Back to reality...

The #HOLISTIC Approach gives the applicant, who comes with some baggage, namely weak grades or test scores, another platform to #SHINE. These kinds of students are the dreamers, who live *outside the conventional box* and create their own paths. These are the #SELFMOTIVATED kids that have above average intelligence. In truth, these are the kinds of applicants all universities and Schools want in the 21st century.

REMEMBER: A College advisor and guidance counselor will be helpful to advise how best to showcase this Extraordinary skill set throughout the application.

The Holistic approach is still a huge gamble. The applicant faces a major uphill climb and the Vegas odd are still #SLIMTONOCHANCE of getting accepted. When I hear 'Holistic Approach', I visualize a highway that is brightly lighted and lined with fluffy clouds to soften a very rocky road to a potential acceptance. My fantasy to soften the reality of #REJECTION.

The Holistic Approach is the furthest thing from 'easy', and it takes a huge effort on the part of the parent and student to best convey the Extraordinary, Unique qualities that distinguish this 'soft applicant' from the others around them, so buckle up!

Holistic applicants must minimize their weaknesses, such as a bad grade in calculus and 'explain them away'. Yes, you better come up with a great excuse why the grade was bad. And no, you cannot use the excuse that your dog ate your homework every night. Then, you start the *Holistic Tap Dance* and showcase your strengths and unique skill set, to obliterate any weakness or wart that stands out on your application.

REMEMBER: The guidance counselor is the only person that can make a desperate attempt to explain away a bad grade. Yes, you can say I prayer if it makes you feel better, although it may not be answered.

Regardless of the existence of an applicant's Extraordinary skill, many Elite Schools still expect their admission requirements be met. Thus, the Schools advisors do not like to sell the Holistic angle to students. It takes tremendous effort to *package* a Holistic applicant and sell this kid to the Dean. #LONGSHOT #NOGUARANTEE.

Do you really think a private College advisor wants to sell you the false hope of getting your kid accepted to an Elite Schools? Many advisors and counselors may not want to do so, because the Vegas odds are against the applicant. They would prefer just to get your kid into the safe school and call it a day.

Lastly, advisors prefer not to roll the dice and take a swing at the Holistic Approach, because it goes against their mantra that an applicant must meet the criteria threshold required by Admissions. These advisors view Elite admissions through a black and white lens, where there is no gray, Holistic area. Simply stated, an applicant is either #ACCEPTED OR #REJECTED.

Needless to say, after meeting with the College advisor we were #OVERWHELMED. Just a wee bit. I hate getting a dose of reality and this meeting was a full serving of it. If I took what the advisor had said as law, there was no chance of my son getting accepted to an Elite School.

But there was no way in hell that I was going to listen to the advisor. I was determined to get my son accepted to the Elite Schools he wanted, and I would make sure the advisor would help me do it. Listen, to know me is to love me, and I am a very persistent mama.

The clock was ticking. To me, it sounded more like a gong. It was June and my son had just finished his junior year of high school. #HALLELUJAH. We were about to put set everything into motion and start the College application process. Senior year begins in just two months…

PART 2

COLLEGE ADMISSIONS UNVEILED: WHAT THE DEAN OF UNDERGRADUATE ADMISSIONS WANTS IN AN APPLICANT!

A dmissions is not known for its transparency. Rather, the review of a candidate's application for admission is highly #SECRETIVE. This creates a bit of a problem.

We just do not know what the Dean is specifically looking for in a candidate in *any given year*. My fellow parents, you need to look into your crystal ball to figure out what qualities the dean is looking for in applicants in your kid's admission year. If you have an idea what the Dean wants in applicants, you may be able to make an educated guess if your kid has any chance in hell to get accepted.

When the admissions committee is reviewing applications, we are left on the outside, clueless as to *how* they decide who gets accepted. We can only *speculate* as to the specific type of applicant the Elite School is looking for, not the specific traits that the Dean has on the radar for this given year. This is simply not fair #OHSHIT!

I would prefer to minimize the guessing and be on the same page as the Dean for specific application requirements each year. The only problem is that I am not a fortune teller or a psychic.

To figure out what kind of applicant the Dean is looking for we need to 'pretend' that we are a Dean of Undergraduate Admissions at the Elite Schools our kid wants to attend. Let us walk in their shoes... First off, these Deans are 'just like us,' they have kids and are confronted by the same problems we encounter. I have met a Dean or two, and I will confess, they are genuinely nice people. Really. They are likable, and they do have a sense of humor. That said, if they reject you, there is nothing funny about it.

Of course, it is trivial whether the Dean is nice or funny. I am merely trying to #HUMANIZE the Dean, and to remove any image of this person sitting in a high tower with long red, velvet robes and who you may perceive can ruin, or derail your child's future.

To some degree, this imagining isn't hyperbolic... your kid's future does rest in their office.

Let's cut to the chase. Since we do not know the Dean, we will not be able walk in their shoes. What is the next best thing?

Go online, and research Interviews with the Dean of Undergraduate Admissions at the Elite Schools your kid aspires to attend.

Specifically, look for interviews where the Dean discusses the most recent applicant pool. The Dean may discuss the type of students that make up previous class years and how the Schools looks to the future. Read #BETWEENTHELINES during these interviews. You may unearth a tiny pearl of wisdom revealed by the Dean...

THE DEAN OF UNDERGRADUATE ADMISSIONS SCULPTS EACH ENTERING FRESHMAN CLASS

This brings me to the second part of this book—when our kids actually apply to Elite Schools. *The applicant must know their target audience.* An applicant is applying for a position in a first-year class; thus, they must be armed with the right pitch to #SELLTHEMSELVES. In this instance the Dean is the #TARGETAUDIENCE.

Let's cut to the chase, again. Parents and applicants must know what *attributes* the Dean is looking for in applicants during the *current* admission cycle. Due to the ridiculous number of applicants, the completed application must be accomplished with significant forethought to captivate the attention of the Dean.

#WISEWORDS: My fellow parents, it is not what the Elite School can do for your kid, rather what your kid can do for the Elite School.

Each new admission cycle, the Dean builds a new first-year class with the foresight of enhancing the sustainability and future of the Institution. It is the expectation that the admitted student will continue to develop their extraordinary talents on campus and contribute to a robust campus community.

That, my friends, is the #BIGPICTURE of what the Dean wants!

CHAPTER 17

THE COLLEGE ADMISSIONS PROCESS

#B URNINGQUESTION... How does a College admissions office read over 40,000 applications for only 1,700 spots in the incoming first-year class? In truth, prior to my kids applying to Elite Institutions, I had no idea.

Personally, I find the world of applying to Elite Schools fascinating. To the unwitting parent and applicant, admissions is cloaked in #SECRECY and we are #CLUELESS as to how applications are scrutinized. Oh, to be a fly on the wall during closed door admissions committee review! So exciting! Not! Just go with it. I'm trying to lighten the mood in this very *high* anxiety filled time.

Based on countless discussions with admissions officers, guidance counselors, and Schools advisors throughout the years, I have learned that applications are in fact #REVIEWED.

As the sun rises and sets each day, a real live person reads each application. Admitted students will have their application read four to five times. In some ways, I found that #COMFORTING.

The amount of effort that goes into submitting just one application can be torture! Damn right they better read that masterpiece. And yes, by the time we finish 'packaging' that application it will be a #MASTERPIECE.

Much to my dismay, however, one friend told me that an Elite School will toss an application if the transcript does not reflect straight A's throughout high school. #GOODBYEAPPLICANT. Now, that is frightening news for parents who are already nervous wrecks.

This is just another reason your kid must be a Qualified applicant when he or she applies to any Schools. Do not waste your time if your kid is not Qualified. If you do so, which I am confident you will, it will be at your own risk!

The following is how Admissions reviews applicants…take notes!

ADMISSIONS ASKS: IS YOUR STUDENT A QUALIFIED APPLICANT?

Finally, the time has arrived to apply to an Elite School. Hooray! Up to this moment, we have been *deliberately* shaping a student for several years to be a Qualified applicant.

When we attended those College tours, admission officers told prospective students the application requirements, specifically the grades and board scores required by each school.

These were the #MINIMALREQUIREMENTS to be a Qualified applicant. Yes, the *low-end* of what admissions requires.

Do you think anyone really 'listened' to these rigorous admission requirements? Hell no! Most of the audience turned a deaf ear. Prospective applicants acknowledged the grades and standardized test score requirements and then, despite not meeting the specific admissions criteria, still applied to the Elite Schools. If they did apply, they were #REJECTED.

REMEMBER: Admissions informs all applicants of the application requirements via information sessions, the Schools website, and Schools reference books.

THERE ARE NO GUARANTEES THAT A QUALIFIED APPLICANT WILL GET ACCEPTED TO AN ELITE SCHOOLS!

Despite your efforts, there are absolutely #NOGUARANTEES that you can pull this rabbit out of the hat to secure an acceptance to the Colleges of your kid's dreams. Even if your kid has perfect scores and grades, he or she may be lacking in another component of the application.

BAD NEWS: If this happens their application will be tossed. #REJECTED

GOOD NEWS: If your kid is a Qualified Applicant, you can try.

◆ ◆ ◆

HOLD UP...

Please take a moment to realize just how easily we can get swept into the Elite School mania. You must admit that at times this entire process can and does border on the absurd.

#WISEWORDS: An illness can be fatal, getting rejected from an Elite School is not.

RANDOM SELECTION PROCESS: A
ROLL OF THE DICE

Despite having zero control. I will give you a few #TIPS to maneuver the mysterious admissions process. As an outsider looking in, you cannot help but wonder what really happens when admission officers sit together and review applications. Do they sit in a large conference room? Do they read portions of essays aloud? Do they make jokes about the chutzpah that some applicants had when they applied? Do they cry when they read sad life stories? How do they process multiples of tens of thousands of applications? They are, in fact, #ONLYHUMAN.

The following IRL exemplifies how the rules of the game are changed at the behest of the applicant...

An Elite School hosts a prestigious summer program, which accepts an extremely limited amount of elite rising high school seniors. The kids perceive this program to be a priceless opportunity to be part of a unique learning opportunity, in addition to building their resume. At the conclusion of the program, admission officers and the program administrators encourage the kids to apply ED to this School in the fall.

◆ ◆ ◆

HOLD UP...

Yes, this really happened. The Kool-Aid was served, chilled to perfection, and the kids drank it. It was incredibly *enticing* to these kids because in prior years, the College accepted a large percentage of alumni from this summer program. These kids eagerly and obediently applied ED to this Elite School. I would have done the same. So, what do you think happened? Did these super smart, accomplished kids get accepted? #HELLNO #NOTTHATYEAR!

In fact, most of the kids who attended that program were #REJECTED. #SHOCKING! The previous year, many of the attendees of that program who had applied ED were accepted as incoming first-year students. For whatever reason, this College chose to *snub* the applicants, or, should I say, the kids *felt* they were snubbed. They were let down, and woefully disappointed. Of course, the following year most of the kids who attended the same summer program were accepted to the Schools. #WTF!?

Since I had a front row seat to watching this whole mess unfold, many of the kids believed this summer program erred in their approach to encourage them to apply to their Elite School. First, these kids #WASTED their one and only early decision application on this school. Second, and I will say this in a 'nice way,' these kids were misinformed by admissions. Let us be serious here and understand what transpired...

The kids who attended this Elite College summer program were all incredibly talented, highly intelligent, Qualified and *over*-Qualified rising seniors from all over the world. At the end of the summer program, after living in the dorms, wearing the College apparel, and utilizing all that the College offered to further their summer studies, these kids were fully immersed in the ethos of this College. They felt as if they too were already a matriculated College student. Of course they felt that way, and we did not expect anything less.

When admission officers met with them, and encouraged them all to apply to this School, these naïve kids got sucked into the vortex of false hope. Based on the representations made by the 'powers that be' of the program and this college, the kids applied ED with the #EXPECTATION they would get accepted. Under these circumstances, anyone would believe this statement. Why wouldn't you follow this directive?

This is a #POWERFUL lesson to be learned. Applicants should loosely follow the statistics from the previous accepted first-year class.

#WISEWORDS: It is clear the rubric changes from year to year. This partly explains why the high school senior who is considered a #PERFECTCANDIDATE can be rejected, accepted, or wait listed.

There are simply more Qualified, and I even dare to say, *over*-Qualified applicants than there are spots in an incoming first-year class.

Due to the *exceptional* qualification of applicants, there appears to be no rhyme or reason as to why Qualified kids are accepted and, conversely, rejected. There are just not enough seats.

Here is the deal my fellow parents. I will attempt to explain in simple English in the next few chapters, how applications are evaluated in the context of what the *Dean wants*.

THE DEAN EVALUATES & COMPARES APPLICANTS WITHIN THE CONTEXT OF THEIR HIGH SCHOOL

For anxious high school seniors who have the singular focus of getting accepted to an Elite School, it is very easy to get lulled into a #FALSE sense of security while applying. This can happen when students look to the previous years' acceptance rates to these Elite Colleges and Universities from their respective high schools.

As we discussed earlier in the book, top-notch public and private high schools often boast consistent acceptance rates and perpetuate the expectation that their school is a #FEEDERSCHOOL to Elite Colleges and Universities.

Once again, there are no guarantees as to the exact number of feeder-school acceptances to be offered for each admissions cycle. It can vary. #OHSHIT! Moreover, the higher the Elite University or College ranking, the more likely that students from an Elite high school will apply.

This means one high school could have fifteen students apply. This is utterly ridiculous. Seriously, how many students do you think will get accepted? 15? 10? 5? 0 students? *Maybe* 2 or 4 students will get accepted, maybe less. Only the Dean knows that answer.

In this situation, it is my expectation and hope that the high school's College advisor would have counseled all 15 students prior to their applying ED to the *same* school.

These students needed to be advised that in addition to competing with the ED applicants from around the world, their *immediate, ultimate* competition is with their own high school classmates. #SURVIVALOFTHEFITTEST.

As you should understand by now, since there are a finite number of first-year seats and a high global demand, there is absolutely #NOWAY 15 kids from the same high school would *all* get accepted ED.

In this regard, for the students that are either *not* a Fit for this College, or are simply *not* Qualified, this would be a #WASTE of an ED application. Please do NOT *throw away* the ED choice!

THE DEAN EVALUATES APPLICANTS WITHIN THE CONTEXT OF THEIR GEOGRAPHICAL LOCATION

Let's continue with the example of fifteen students applying ED to the same Elite College or University. The next item that the Dean at this Elite School will review is whether there are other ED applicants from the same geographic location. This not only includes applicants from other public and private high schools in that town, but also applicants from the same city, neighboring towns, the county, and the entire state.

I would not go as far as to say there are 'feeder states,' although I do believe that Elite Schools have a few states that cultivate a larger percentage of acceptances. There must be limits as to how many Qualified and overqualified students are accepted from one state.

Elite Schools want to accept Qualified students from every state in the U.S., and from countries throughout the world. That being said, the Deans wants highly intelligent, Qualified applicants from less populated states. Too many kids apply to Elite schools from NY, CA, NJ, FL, TX, and the home state of the Schools. This can result in way too many overqualified applicants from the usual suspect states, who will get rejected because they are #GEOGRAPHIC-ALLYUNDESIRABLE".

You know this term from the days of dating. A person can be a great 'catch' but considered to be a 'GUD".

If you really are a 'really' #SMARTANDSAVVY parent, before your kid starts high school, move to North Dakota.

CHAPTER 18

THE ADMISSIONS OFFICE RUBRIC

Deans throughout this country utilize a grading system to expeditiously review the tens of thousands of Schools applicants their offices receive each admission cycle. Once Admissions determines an applicant is Qualified, the Dean formulates a Rubric that identifies and quantifies whether the Qualified applicant meets or exceeds the requirement to be #COMPELLING.

The Rubric is composed of specific objective and subjective requirements for acceptance. It is a checklist of sorts unique to each Elite Schools, formulated by the Dean to evaluate applicants.

These requirements are assessed by a Rating System. Each requirement for admission is scored from 0 (lowest requirement achievement) to a 5 (requirement fully achieved.) The rubric varies at each Elite College. The goal is to score the #MAXIMUM amount of points allotted in each category. This is how the body of work and life of the applicant from 9th grade to present day is rated.

REMEMBER…the Dean sculpts an incoming first-year class that will *embody* the Institution's current and future vision.

THE RUBRIC REQUIREMENTS ARE AS FOLLOWS:

1. Transcript, Test Scores. A caveat to this first requirement: failure to meet admission requirements for Grades, GPA, Curriculum and Standard Test Scores will result #REJECTED. Do not pass go, do not go to the 2nd Rubric Requirement;

2. The ENGAGED Applicant (EC's);

3. The ESSAYS;
4. The COMPELLING Applicant.

Based on the limited number of seats available in every incoming class, the Dean selects an applicant they expect will #FLOURISH in their school's community.

#WISEWORDS: When Deans makes their final decision, they look for #SYNERGY between the applicants *poised* for acceptances.

The goal at Elite Schools is for the students to work together and #COLLABORATE not only on a personal level for self-fulfillment, but also for the greater good of their classmates and community.

HOW THE DEAN ALLOCATES ACCEPTANCES

This is the part of the book that I hope will further clarify how difficult it is to get accepted to an Elite School. We have already established that the applicant pool grows exponentially each new admissions cycle, and that no two admission years are the same.

Thus, I believe the Dean formulates a new strategy at the beginning of each admissions cycle to guide the selection process for the incoming first year class. Applicants are divided into "groups", where each group is allocated a specific amount of acceptances, which is a percentage of the entire applicant pool. It all adds up to 100%!

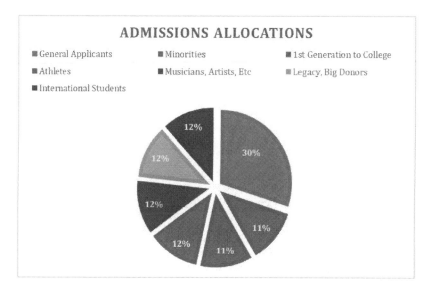

Here we go! When allocating percentages to different applicant groups, it is necessary to use a pie chart. #TAKENOTES....

Out of 100% of applicants, the percent allocation is as follows:

1. The first 10-12% of admitted applicants goes to International Students;

2. The second 10-12% of admitted applicants goes to Minority Students;

3. The third 10-12% of admitted applicants goes to First Generation Schools Students;

4. The fourth 10-15% of admitted applicants goes to Athletes

5. The fifth 10-12% of admitted applicants goes to wherever there are specific vacancies in the first-year class (i.e. the orchestra, band, artists, etc.)

6. The sixth 10-12% of admitted applicants goes to Legacy and Donor families.

7. The remainder of the class, roughly 25-30% of admitted applicants gets distributed amongst the rest of the students who are trying to get into the school.

Let us analyze the chart. By the time admissions is done allotting percentages to so many diverse applicant groups, the Regular Applicant pool is where our kid will vie for a spot. Our kid is the Not that Kid ('NOTKID'), who is the student defined by their negatives in comparison to other applicants reflected in the chart—they are not the drummer, not the legacy, not the daughter of a big donor, not the actress, not a minority, and not a first-generation College student in the family.

The NOTKID, is your kid. Here is an IRL that explains percentage allocations. At the beginning of a new admission cycle for 1,750 first-year seats, the Dean allocates the percentages for acceptance for this class. The NOTKID is left vying for the remaining 425 to 500 first-year seats out of an admission pool of over 40,000 applicants. Perhaps this puts into perspective just how difficult it is to get accepted to an Elite School. The odds: #SLIMTONOCHANCE.

When we discuss allocation percentages, I would be remiss not to address the alumni and donors. All Colleges and Universities appreciate and love their alumni and donors for their spiritual camaraderie... and their financial support. Donations are the means through which these Schools not only ensure their institution's survival, but also continue to update and modernize their campus and hire the best and brightest minds to propel the institution forward. These continuous improvements benefit both current and future students by providing a secondary education that gives them the opportunity to achieve personal success.

But these many bells and whistles are not the only things Elite Schools strive to provide through the use of alumni dollars. Elite Schools also use their funding to hire professors best positioned to have the most profound and positive impact on a student. Great professors are 'lured' to Elite Institutions and, trust me, this costs money. Donations make this happen. Yes, donations can be a big deal. It is, the substantial and consistent donations that will at a minimum, *get the applicant on the school's radar, not guarantee acceptance.*

Based on my pie chart, there are not that many spots available to alumni and donors who are jockeying their kids to get accepted. It is my presumption that in addition to donations, the applicant must still be Qualified and Compelling, in addition to meeting the Dean's requirements to be accepted.

The real kicker in this equation is for the applicant to be Qualified. Despite generous donations, I do not believe that un-Qualified applicants will get accepted.

REMEMBER: We want our kids to flourish on an intellectual and emotional level as they mature. Elite Schools are a place where like-minded, brilliant students are encouraged not only to challenge themselves and their classmates on an academic level, but to inspire each other in a collaborative effort.

CHAPTER 19

THE FIRST RUBRIC:

GRADES AND STANDARDIZED
TEST SCORES

When your kid submits their College application, it is officially in the hands of the Office of Undergraduate Admissions. The entire application will be reviewed in accordance with the Rubric that was tailor made by the Dean at that Elite College or University. Failure to meet each component of the Rubric results in #REJECTION.

The applicant must pass the first rubric of admissions, which is a comprehensive review of the transcript and standardized test scores.

THE DEAN WANTS A TRANSCRIPT THAT EVIDENCES THE HARDEST CLASSES

The transcript is the first document reviewed by the Dean. Unbeknownst to most people, the transcript tells the applicant's story about academics, fortitude, and intelligence.

The Dean wants to see applicants who were challenged academically. The transcript shows a 4-year history of straight 'A's received in the hardest curriculum offered at their respective high school. Perfection is a #BITCH!

When the applicant is a first semester senior, the transcript should resemble a #MASTERPIECE of superior grades and honors courses. Yes indeed, a beautiful work of art, that was strategically planned by the guidance counselor since the applicant's first day of high school.

#WISEWORDS: If your kid's transcript does not satisfy the minimum academic requirements of an Elite School by their senior year, they should not apply. Why? They will get #REJECTED.

REMEMBER: CHAPTER 16.

THE DEAN WANTS SPECIFIC REQUIRED COURSES FOR ADMISSION

In addition to expecting students to take the most rigorous high school classes, the Dean requires all Elite applicants to have taken specific high school courses to make it past the first rubric.

For example, if the Dean requires applicants to take AP Calculus in high school, it is required that course be on the Transcript. Non-honors calculus will not fly. If you have not completed the expected requirements, do not bother applying. These are Elite admission requirements and every applicant must adhere to them. There are #NOEXCEPTIONS.

REALTALK: Will one or two non-honors classes ruin your child's chances of being a proper applicant to a select school? The answer is, maybe. I know this is not the answer any parent wants to hear, but it is the truth.

Personally, I believe Elite Schools would prefer to see that your kid took the honors math class and received a 'B', rather than take the non-honors class. In this circumstance, you would hope that your student's application is reviewed #HOLISTICALLY so that the Dean can see the intellectual depth and fortitude of the student that is evidenced throughout their transcript.

ADMISSIONS GPA AND TEST SCORE RANGES

The weighted/unweighted GPA range is 3.8 to 5.0. The ACT range is 32-36, and the SAT is 1450-1600. The Dean's prefers the applicant to be at the high end of these ranges. Why does the Dean care about the transcript and test scores? The Dean believes this data is #PREDICTIVE of the overall academic performance of a matriculated first-year student. Failure to meet the minimum range requirement #REJECTION.

THE DEAN EVALUATES HOW AN APPLICANT CONFRONTS ADVERSITY

My fellow parents, do you remember when we discussed the pitfalls associated with 'rewarding failure' in Chapter 10? The Dean wants to know how resilient an applicant can be when faced with #ADVERSITY.

In a situation where a student drops the AP Calc class in favor of a non-honors class to secure an 'easy A', this move might #BACKFIRE if the Elite School's overall applicant pool is *over*-Qualified.

Adversity occurs when we are pushed to any limit. If your student has *not challenged* themselves, it will be difficult to have any examples that demonstrate the strength of their resiliency and or spirit to the Dean. The question is always, "Can we motivate ourselves to surpass that limit?"

#WISEWORDS: Sometimes, #ADVERSITY can result in personal growth due to our resiliency to achieve.

When an adolescent is academically challenged (perhaps for the first time) do not despair! The glass is always full baby! When conveyed strategically, this event can be portrayed to the Dean as a life changing advancement. I am confident you, my fellow parent, never thought of that!

Despite receiving a lower grade in the AP Calc class that your student 'hobbled through' all year, they could still use this event in the College essay to address the way they *adapt* to challenging experiences (refer to Chapter 26).

REMEMBER: The guidance counselor could help 'explain away' this grade in their personal assessment of the student.

THE DEAN MAY REWARD ACADEMIC CHALLENGES WITH A BROWNIE POINT

The Dean wants to know how the applicant *confronted* challenges and failures. For some students, there does come a point when 'the coasting through life' comes to an abrupt halt. The Dean wants to know how you managed that sudden, dramatic event. Did your kid address it head on, or did your kid *run away*?

If I were a betting mom, and I am, my guess is that the Dean wants to hear the story of an applicant who stared defeat in the eye and found a way to move past this challenge. It is this kind of applicant that can earn a #BROWNIEPOINT from the Dean.

#WISEWORDS: We all get more out of life when we go outside of our comfort zone. Sometimes we create self-imposed boundaries intended to shield us from any challenge that could make us feel even a wee bit uncomfortable.

STANDARDIZED TESTS: THE SAT AND ACT

As we know, standardized tests are not much fun. The good news is there is a new trend, ever so small, that some Colleges and Universities no longer require the submission of standardized test scores. #HOORAY! #FREEDOM!

These Schools refer to their admission requirements as #TESTOPTIONAL.

The GOOD NEWS: This is true. The applicant is not required to submit scores.

The BAD NEWS: Most Elite Schools still require a standardized test score. If your student plans to apply to an Elite School, they are out of luck and must study to take either the SAT or ACT.

Standardized tests are College entrance exams meant to measure the College readiness of an applicant. The SAT is part of the 'College Board' company, who is the creator of the exams most parents have grown to hate such as the SAT, SAT Subject Tests, and AP exams. The ACT is not owned by the College Board and is a different readiness exam. I am not going to describe the SAT and the ACT, nor will I divulge my preference.

All of these standardized tests #SUCK.

The pressure on students to attain high test scores is ludicrous. Schools want these scores because it is another way to *differentiate* the growing applicant pool. Extensive test preparation is a necessary means to the end of getting a high score, which costs big bucks. We are not talking about a few hundred dollars, but thousands of dollars to pay for study classes or a private tutor.

Most high school students require several months of studying to take these exams. Test prep can start as early as 10th grade., although typically starts in the fall of 11th grade for most students. In addition to regular schoolwork, test prep should be done every day, with practice test taking on the weekends.

Test prep eats up any extra time the already overloaded, overworked, and overwhelmed high school junior could possibly have for themselves. It takes away study time juniors need for AP and honors classes, as well as after school sports and activities.

For the kids that want to attend an Elite School, the junior year is not the time for a social life. There is just no time #SADBUTTRUE.

The ultimate problem of standardized tests is that a perfect test score *does not guarantee* acceptance to an Elite Schools. There are simply too many *over-*Qualified applicants, so the selection process has become more random and less certain.

The ACT and SAT exams are offered 3 to 4 times per academic year. Each exam is composed of several sections. Each section is scored individually, which forms the basis of the overall test score, known as the composite score. Most Elite Schools want to see every standardized test ever taken, which is reflected in the 'Score Report'.

The Deans do encourage students to take these tests 2 to 3 times, although they have observed that most students do not experience much change in their test scores between the second and third time.

SUPER SCORING!

I love super scoring! There you go, one bright spot with these tests. For many kids, if they take these tests several times, their scores can or may vary on each individual section. Welcome to 'Super Scoring'. When your kid is a roller coaster test taker, meaning there is no predictable, consistent composite score, some Schools permit applicants to super score their tests.

Hallelujah for super scoring! This is one of the few times you may just get a break with these exams. Super scoring allows you to #CHERRYPICK the best individual test score of each section of the exam, to create a 'super scored' single test.

Most Deans request *all* tests be submitted in their entirety and do not permit super scoring. Yes, the Deans will see the good, the bad, and the ugly of all the test scores.

Now I do not want to instill fear in you. Standardized tests are incredibly #STRESSFUL. So much so, I can often imagine why some parents pay to have their students' tests taken for them. *THIS IS NEVER AN OPTION.* Do not become one of them.

Please breathe. This standardized testing stuff is complicated, overwhelming, and for some, expensive, but it is never worth jeopardizing your kid's intellectual integrity, and your personal freedom. #VARSITYBLUES.

Parents and students must understand and appreciate just how difficult it is to apply to Elite Schools. The applicant cannot even get their foot in the door for consideration to be reviewed by Admissions if they do not have the required grades and scores. Even when the first requirement is met, there are still other components of the rubric that are equally as daunting and challenging.

However, the other criteria are more subjective in nature and seek to highlight the applicant's

#LIFEACCOMPLISHMENTS.

CHAPTER 20

THE SECOND RUBRIC:

THE ENGAGED APPLICANT

As we unveil the admissions process, we learned the first rubric requirement is an objective review of grades and standard test scores. The applicant either meets the minimum requirements for admission or they are rejected. There is very little leeway or compromise.

If the application satisfies the first rubric requirement, the second round is where admissions will conduct an extensive subjective review of the remainder of the application.

These are innate, human qualities the Dean is specifically looking for in each candidate, that will not only define them as unique but will contribute to their College or University community as an active participant. The applicant will proffer subjective data to evidence their Engagement in personal accomplishments and EC's.

#WISEWORDS: The applicant must highlight their personal story to rise above every other applicant and to *distinguish* their Extraordinary, Unique skill set.

The applicant must look inward and do some soul searching to determine whether they are passionate about something in their life. In the context of the Elite admissions world, passion is defined as the applicant's affinity and zeal to pursue a *sincere* love of an endeavor. In this sense, a student's Engagement is synonymous with their Passion.

THE DEAN WANTS AN ENGAGED APPLICANT

The Engagement of an applicant is evidenced through their personal story and extracurricular activities. The key here is that parents should help their inquisitive child find an activity that complements their developing skill sets when they are in elementary and or middle school. All kids benefit from doing something that not only makes them happy, but also gives them a sense of accomplishment.

The Dean will admit that it is the parents' job to provide their kids with opportunities to do the things they love. It is for the kid to ultimately *commit* to an activity and strive to make a difference in their universe. This is not about kids participating in enrichment programs. This is about parents empowering their kids with the opportunity to shine in areas they genuinely love.

Once a kid starts to exhibit a proclivity towards a specific activity, it may evolve into their sole focus for unique personal achievement. In the context of applying to an Elite School, the student must convey this personal story to the admissions committee. Their personal journey will be demonstrated through participation in their EC's which confirm the *evolution* of their unique passion.

#WISEWORDS: A Unique applicant is one whose passion is the focal point of their life, *defines* their individuality and distinguishes them from peers.

When the admissions committee evaluates an application in its entirety between 4 and 5 times, the *voice of the student must* #RESONATE.

PASSION

Let's address Passion. This is such an important word in the context of applying to an Elite Institution. The new buzzwords are "Passion", and/or Engagement.". In the 21st Century, these terms are a critical component to the overall Elite application.

Passion is evidenced by the motivation that drives us to reach for the stars, to create, question, and function #OUTSIDETHEBOX. Passion can be equated as the love of an activity. Passion emanates from the heart, mind, body, and soul. It is not contrived. True passion will be written all over the application. The EC's a student participates in will reflect the embodiment of their passion.

Simply stated, their world revolves around their passion.

Innovation and Entrepreneurship are the forces that drive global industry in the 21st century. Elite Schools have embraced the era of technology and seek applicants who develop apps and technology in their bedrooms. The Dean wants these impassioned dreamers, because they are our future #VISIONAR-IES.

It is imperative that the 21st century College applicant to an Elite School must be Engaged. Applicants must exhibit a legitimate love of something that defines who they are now that is a lens to their future. An Engaged student is #MULTIDIMENSIONAL. Many students can take AP courses, receive straight A's, have a perfect GPA and standard test scores, but not everyone has #PAS-SION.

In the quest to get accepted to an Elite School, you must do something else besides study. Passion just may be the #SECRET WEAPON that catapults a candidate into the final round of application decisions. Perhaps the Dean will admit an aspiring entrepreneur to the incoming first-year class.

THE DEAN WANTS TO KNOW HOW STUDENTS
TAKE ADVANTAGE OF OPPORTUNITIES

The Dean wants students who *know* what to do when #OPPORTUNITY-KNOCKS.

The Dean wants to know if and when students seized or created an opportunity, and what, if any *challenges* sprung up. How did the student address these challenges? This brings us back to the importance of how applicants deal with #ADVERSITY.

How does a student convey to the Dean a genuine passion? Passion is exhibited from countless activities and actions. A competitive tennis player can be passionate about the game of tennis. An impassioned moviegoer may create a web site devoted to their own movie reviews. I may or may not have sons who displayed these endeavors.

#WISEWORDS: Legitimate Passion cannot be photoshopped.

Some students *create* their own opportunities, because none exist in their school or local community.

An IRL of genuine passion in action was where a 12-year-old kid discovered the public library out of sheer boredom. It is true, a library is a great place to get books, but for creative kids, it could be a refuge. Hard to believe life without Netflix, HULU, Spotify, ITUNES, etc., but 10 years ago the internet did not have every song, album, TV show and movie available for daily consumption. Perhaps this kid's initial trips to the library stemmed from boredom, but soon, the resources the library provided allowed his love of music to flourish. In the local library, he not only downloaded thousands of the songs they had on file, but he also ordered tens of thousands of more songs via "Intra-library Lending'. This allowed all libraries in the county to share their entire inventory with each other.

In truth, some of the librarians dreaded the sight of this kid, because he would order at least 40 to 50 albums a week, all of which they had to manually process. However, little did they know, they were fueling his passion. Soon, this kid's passion for music spread to film. The local library proved to be an invaluable resource, which he utilized weekly until he left for College.

Over time, the librarians all greeted him by his first name, and would revel in discussing the films, tv shows, and music he unearthed. In some ways, he became their resource to discover and learn about this medium. This passion manifested itself in his creation of a movie review website, a music company, and a data analytics firm.

At the time, if someone had looked at his EC's, his evolving trajectory towards the arts and technology would have been evident.

Moreover, his personal story was true...

#MOTIVATION #CREATEDOPPORTUNITY #DIDITHIMSELF #ENGAGEMENT #UNIQUE.

This is another example of why it is so important to properly convey on your application your EC's. Remember the kid, Craig, who was deferred? He was the 'all in robotics kid', who imagined protypes of robotic devices he aspired to design and build, to improve our lives. He was 100% sincere in his quest to change the world for the better with robotics. The problem was that he failed to convey that fact on his ED application. Nowhere on that application gave a scintilla of a hint that robotics dominated his life and was the essence of his passion. #BIGMISTAKE.

Most high school students' draft resumes in preparation for completing the Common App. These resumes work to organize their EC's, jobs (AKA career opportunities or internships), awards, sports, etc.

On the other hand, Craig, had a resume that reflected the look and feel of a kid who played with an erector set. I was dumbfounded and, quite frankly, *pissed* that he pulled the trigger and applied ED without writing a compelling essay and application that conveyed his future ambitions. It was clear that he was not advised by any counselor as to how to properly fill out the Common App.

This my fellow parents, should not be repeated by future applicants. I believe the Essay Section is pivotal to the overall success of an application. When Craig re-shaped his Common App, he *eloquently* shared how a learning impairment caused him to work exponentially harder than his peers. It was his passion for creating, developing, and building in robotics that *motivated* him to succeed.

Thus, the College applications he submitted for RA revealed him to be a multi-dimensional candidate bound for future success due to his own determination and ability to overcome #ADVERSITY. In case you were wondering, he was accepted to an Elite University in Regular Admission. As a matter of fact, he just received his Master's degree, and will be pursuing a doctorate degree in, you guessed it, Mechanical Engineering, at an Elite University. #BRAVO#SELFMOTIVATION#EARNEDIT #LOVETHATKID!

I am not a math whiz, but I have created a mathematical equation for the Elite School admission process.

QUALIFED Applicant + PASSION = **COMPELLING** Applicant.

The Compelling application *should* make it to the final rounds of admission. There is one caveat: there are #NOGUARANTEES.

CHAPTER 21

EXTRACURRICULAR ACTIVITIES:

THE DEAN WANTS MULTI-DIMENSIONAL EXTRAORDINARY CANDIDATES

Your kid must stand above and apart from classmates who apply to the same Elite Schools, and ask themselves 'do they want to make an impact in their universe'?

The only chance in hell to even make it to the final rounds of the admissions committee, is to be a Qualified student who possess an *Extraordinary, Multi-Dimensional* skill set that catapults you above your classmates who are all vying to attend the same Elite School.

REMEMBER: If 10 students are applying ED to the same Elite School, only 1 to 2 kids will get accepted. BTW, some years, no one from that school get accepted ED #REALITY #SUCKS.

THE DEAN EMPHASIZES EXTRACURRICULAR AND ACADEMIC ACTIVITIES

Extracurricular Activities, the infamous "EC's", play an integral role in the application process because they define the applicant. The EC's are the activities a student participates in outside of the classroom. Leadership can be a quality that results from participation in EC's. As you will learn, this is another critical component to the application.

In the 21st century, Leaders are considered to be the *Innovative Risktakers* who endeavor to discover new frontiers in science, technology, and business to fundamentally change how we move as a society. Yes, this is a #BIGDEAL.

Leadership can play a particularly significant role for a student who is a borderline candidate for admission.

EC's must *showcase* the *Engagement* of an applicant.

HOW EC'S SHOWCASE AN EXTRAORDINARY CANDIDATE

My fellow parents, you should all know by now that I love my mantra 'Why be ordinary, when you can be Extraordinary". This is where your kid shines as an Engaged Compelling applicant and catches the attention of the Dean.

Based on my experience, when kids pursue the EC's they love to do, they demonstrate a greater commitment and *sincere* enthusiasm.

As it turns out, an EC, whatever the activity may be, can exemplify the true engagement of the applicant. This validates the applicant as #COMPELLING and worthy of #ADMISSION.

EC'S DISTINGUISH THE FOLLOWING UNIQUE QUALITIES:

1. LEADERSHIP;
2. ACHIEVEMENT;
3. PASSION;
4. MOTIVATION;
5. RISKTAKER;
6. COMMUNITY SERVICE;
7. CONSISTENCY

In addition to grades and test scores, the EC's, must portray the applicant as a person who thinks out of the box and steps outside of their comfort zone to achieve the #EXTRAORDINARY.

When EC's are evaluated in their totality, the *evolution* of this passion measures the #ENGAGEMENT of the applicant.

In some instances, where the applicant's grades are 'soft' (not all straight A's), the EC's might just be the reason why an Elite School grants them admission. The review of an Elite application is akin to a seesaw. In this regard, we want to 'tip' the see-saw in our favor.

Extraordinary EC's could potentially tip the application into the #ADMIT pile. The key to the EC's, is to convey a not-so-subtle story about the student. As a parent, I believe it is important for our kids to be multi-dimensional, not one sided. EC'S represent the #EXTRAORDINARY facets of an applicant.

THE DEAN WANTS LEADERS

There are many components that make up EC's, and in turn define the subjective character of the applicant.

LEADERS forge their own path and *create* opportunities.

LEADERSHIP occurs when kids are the *Founders* of a charity or company, or the captain of a team.

LEADERSHIP will confirm the student has a legitimate passion or proclivity for a specific activity. It is especially important that the student pursued all EC's in a leadership capacity, because this is a quality the Dean wants to see in Compelling applicants.

The Dean wants *self-motivated* students. Leaders do not sit around waiting to be told what to do. Leaders move the world forward. #EXTRAORDINARY.

THE DEAN WANTS APPLICANTS WHO IMPACT THEIR COMMUNITY IN THE CONTEXT OF COMMUNITY SERVICE

Community Service is a very important part of the EC list. In addition to reviewing an applicant's love of learning and ability to take advantage of opportunities, the Dean considers the applicant's impact within their community. Does the applicant care about their community? Are they active participants in making it a better place to live? Does the applicant express #COMPASSION towards others?

Why is this important? When an application is being reviewed 4 to 5 times by admission officers, the Dean wants to know how **this** applicant will contribute to their Schools campus community.

#WISEWORDS: Community service cannot be contrived – it must come from the student, not the parent.

Now keep in mind, the 20-hour community service high school requirement gig will unequivocally not satisfy a requisite for an Elite School. The students that are *Founders* of charitable organizations in their community, are considered to be leaders by the Dean, because they saw a deficit in the community and made a #POSITIVECHANGE.

CHAPTER 22

THE THIRD RUBRIC:

THE COMMON APP AND ESSAYS

We have referred to the Common App at length throughout this book, although never fully explained what it is. The Common App is the official College application. Most, if not all, U.S. Schools require applicants to submit the Common App because it is the central repository for the requisite application pedigree questions, official high school transcript, standardized test scores, description of EC's, honors, awards, and recommendations. In addition, the Common App requires the completion of two Essays.

I blame the Common App for creating the ridiculous surge in Elite School applications throughout the U.S. because it has theoretically *simplified* the application process. The Common App is filled out online and submitted with an actual 'click of a button'. The only problem is the cost per application, which can be #PRICEY.

Thus, the simplicity in filling out applications has given the green lights to kids to submit as many applications as they 'want to'.

The only impediments are costs (yes, it adds up), and writing the essays (which may be more of a deterrent).

In addition to the Common App, individual Colleges and Universities require their own admission applications to be completed. This typically entails the completion of supplemental essays. Yes, on its face, the Common App appears to be easy. This is a #JOKE. As with any online application, it can be confusing to fill out.

What happens to many kids is that despite proofreading the application hundreds of times, they still submit their application with mistakes. I am sure you can imagine the state of #EMERGENCY that ensues while attempting to correct a mistake on the submitted application. Who do you call? There is no Common App #HOTLINE-1-800-REJECTED.

The year my older son applied to College was when the Common App was completely revamped and changed. Most of the professionals were concerned this would wreak havoc among the rising seniors, and early reports showed there were issues with this 'new and improved' Common App.

Somehow a proof-readable mistake slipped through the cracks of his application. My son's College advisor and guidance counselor reviewed the application prior to its submission, and no one caught the mistake. It was so bad that he had to contact each admissions department and re-submit an addendum to each College and University via overnight mail. #TERRIFYINGEXPERI-ENCE #UNNECESSARYDRAMA.

The advent of the Common App has doubled, if not tripled, the number of Qualified applicants that apply to the same Elite Schools. This lowers the acceptance rate, also known as the 'yield.'

Once again you ask, "Why do so many kids apply to these Elite Schools?" It is always the same answer. Tens of thousands of students #FANTASIZE about the perceived lifetime opportunity to attend an Elite U.S. College or University, and there seems to be a universal belief that there is no downside to submitting multiple applications. The chant is, "You have nothing to lose but the application fee." This is true. #EVERYONE wants to be forever associated with an Elite Schools.

This book will not address the several components of the Common App #YOURWELCOME. The most important component of the Common App are the Essays.

THE COMMON APP ESSAYS

We have arrived at the required College essays. The Common App provides infamous essay prompts. Currently, there are 7 prompts the applicant can choose from to write the one Common App required Essay.

The Essay provides a platform, in conjunction with the EC's, for the applicant to tell the Dean, their personal narrative of overcoming Adversity, creating Opportunities, and embodying Leadership in their Community or their Unique approach to Innovation and Entrepreneurship. The essay is the vehicle to tell the Dean they are indeed *the* #COMPELLINGAPPLICANT.

In addition to the Common App essay, Elite Schools have additional application requirements that include supplemental essay prompts.

WRITING COLLEGE ESSAYS...
AN ACQUIRED SKILL

Just to be clear, an applicant does not simply read the prompt and then bang out an essay. #OHNO! The essay responses are *deliberate* in thought. There is a certain way to write these essays. The key is to ensure that the essay catches the eye of the reader. The written responses to each essay prompt are very time consuming and can take months to complete. Moreover, each essay must be proofread by an English teacher, guidance counselor, or College advisor prior to submission.

THE DEAN WANTS ESSAYS THAT ARE
AUTHENTIC AND INTERESTING!

Unbeknownst to most applicants, the Common App essay serves a significant purpose. You just cannot get away from this fact.

The Dean has specific expectations for the applicant's personal narrative and want to see those expectations reflected in 650 words or less.

The Dean wants the essay to convey what *matters* to the applicant. As far as I am concerned, the essay should be a #MASTERPIECE.

A short and sweet response to an essay prompt, written in the precise voice the Dean requires.

THE DEAN WANTS TO HEAR THE APPLICANT'S VOICE RESONATE THROUGHOUT THE ESSAY!

And just what *voice* does the Dean want to hear?

Good question; thank you for asking. When admission officers read essays, they often lament that the voice that resonates throughout the essay is not that of the applicant but sounds like the parent's voice. This is #BAD. Along with their voice, the essay has the parent's fingerprints all over it (grammar, diction, word choice, etc.) and the highly trained officers know the parents wrote the essay! You do not have to be Detective Columbo to figure this out.

Obviously, admission officers can easily discern the difference between a parents' and students' writing styles. I mean, they only read tens of thousands of essays a year, so they have good practice at sniffing out who wrote the essay.

#WISEWORDS: Parents should *absolutely not* write their child's essay.

In fact, parents should not be involved with the essay. The applicant must write the essay in their own #VOICE, in the voice they use when speaking with friends. This is how Admissions gets a feel for the applicant.

#WISEWORDS: The applicant should only write with words they are comfortable using in everyday speech.

For example, do not use the thesaurus… those adjectives are easily caught by admissions, and these colorful, 'fluffy' words get in the way of the writing. Moreover, the Dean knows the Qualified student can write, that skill is *expected*.

#FYI: Writing ability will not get assessed unless the essay is *terrible*.

In addition to the Common App Essay, many Colleges require supplemental essays.

In this instance, an Elite School will require 1 supplemental essay, and an optional 2nd essay. If your kid applies to more than one College and/or University, he or she could have to write upwards of 20 essays. That is a daunting task and is time consuming. Yes, our kids do this.

Listen carefully: *Months* need to be set aside to learn how to write the Schools essays, and to submit the finished product.

REMEMBER: When a student gets rejected or deferred from the ED round, they will to #SCRAMBLE to literally 'bang' out all the essays the Regular Admission Colleges and Universities require in *only* 2 weeks.

This book will *not* provide examples of how essays should be drafted, nor will it give you the 'Do's and Don'ts' for writing the essay. My suggestion is to have your kid ask for direction from the English teacher, guidance counselor or College advisor. If you can, it is well advised to hire a private writing advisor to oversee the extensive editing process of these essays. As a matter of fact, all of the above team members should proof-read the essays.

CHAPTER 23

THE FOURTH RUBRIC:

THE COMPELLING APPLICANT

My fellow brethren. #OYVEY! This is a lot of information for you to process. The admission process to Elite Schools is daunting. Any normal person would believe that perfect grades and standardized test scores would be more than enough to get any smart kid accepted. Any Schools yes, but not Elite Schools. We are dealing with a totally different #BEAST.

I am trying to be methodical in my identification and explanation of the individual components that are integral for admissions to review an application. At first glance, it seems so easy. However, there are just so many moving parts to this complicated process that it is essential parents understand what the Dean wants in an applicant.

THE DEAN WANTS A QUALIFIED APPLICANT WHO IS COMPELLING!

Just *imagine*... your kid applied to an Elite School and you are all waiting for decision day, physically wringing your hands in desperation. Unbeknownst to you, the Admissions Committee has reviewed your kid's application and determined that your kid, yes, your baby, is a Qualified and Engaged Applicant. #OMG!

To confirm, the grades, test scores, and EC's satisfied the first, second and third Rubric Requirements. Pinch me, this is unbelievable!

Do you remember when you prayed every time your kid took a standard test, AP or IB test, final exam, mid-term, blah blah blah? Well mama, your prayers were answered. Big #HALLELUJAH!

The funny part is you have no idea that your kid made it to the admissions fourth round of review. Of course, you have no idea, because it is a secret! Shhhh! Admissions does not contact your kid to give an 'atta boy' or 'atta girl' that they made it to the #FOURTHROUND.

We have arrived at yet another defining moment in this book. Once Admissions classifies the applicant as Qualified, the admission committee will determine whether your kid is a #COMPELLINGAPPLICANT by reading the entire application at least 4 to 5 times.

Thereafter, the Dean will then determine if the applicant is a #FIT for their College.

THE DEAN WANTS A COMPELLING APPLICANT WHO WILL ENHANCE THEIR COLLEGE COMMUNITY

In the Fourth-Round, when the admissions committee is reading through the application, they determine if the applicant will #CONTRIBUTE to their Schools community. Specifically, admissions wants to know: 1) Whether the applicant is Compelling; and 2) What the applicant can bring to this #CAMPUSCOMMUNITY?

THE DEAN CONSIDERS THE INDIVIDUALITY OF EACH APPLICANT

You are not 'special' or unique just because you are smart, took super hard classes, and boast a few extracurricular activities.

As we discussed, the First Round of admissions is based on an objective standard whereby Elite Schools require applicants to take the hardest classes their high school offers, receive top grades, have superior GPA's and near perfect standardized tests scores.

When these applicants make it to the Second and Third Rounds for review, the selection process becomes *personal*, more subjective.

Admissions looks beyond the scores and makes a real effort to determine whether the applicant is *unique*, will be an *active* participant in the school community, and, just maybe, *impact* our world.

Yes parents, this is how the Dean evaluates whether a Qualified applicant is Compelling.

THE DEAN DOES NOT COMPARE STUDENTS TO EACH OTHER

Again, this is about the #INDIVIDUALITY of the student. When applications are reviewed in the latter admission rounds, the Dean does not compare students to each other. In the fourth-round, the student *must* show an Extraordinary skill set to #DISTINGUISH him or herself from the rest of the applicant pool.

This is where the big fish leaps out of the pond to sing the loudest to grab the

Dean's attention!

THE DEAN CONSIDERS THE CURRENT
NEEDS OF THE INSTITUTION

The Dean creates each new entering first-year class in the context of the *current needs* of the Institution. This is a real balancing act that determines which applicants promote and further the present needs of the College and its Community.

THE DEAN WANTS TO KNOW HOW THE
APPLICANT WILL BENEFIT FROM THIS
COLLEGE CAMPUS COMMUNITY

Yes, the Community of the Elite Institution is that important to the Dean.

It is the savvy applicant who discloses to the Dean why this Elite college is a #PERFECTFIT.

The applicant must convey to the Dean that their campus #CULTURE offers a sense of Community and support to students that sets it apart from comparable Institutions.

THE DEAN WANTS TO KNOW WHY THE
APPLICANT LOVES THIS ELITE COLLEGE

#SPECIFICITY is key. The applicant must zero in on their specific academic interests, identify faculty, programs, and courses that are relevant to their interests.

A Tale of Two Applicants:

Why Can Two Similarly Situated Applicants Have Different Admission Outcomes?

Here is an example that answers why similarly situated applicants that apply to the *same* two Elite Schools are either accepted or rejected. One student is accepted to one School, and not the other.

Why does this happen? How can it be that two students who both share the same Qualifications and are Compelling applicants, may not be accepted to the same College?

THE ANSWER: is that it depends upon what the Dean is looking for *in* an applicant and determine which candidate will not only be an integral component of the Schools community, but of the overall institution. This is #BIGSTUFF.

HOW TO CATAPULT A QUALIFIED, COMPELLING APPLICANT INTO THE ADMIT PILE!

Applicants should ask themselves the following questions to *distinguish* themselves from other applicants:

1. *Why* should this Elite Institution *Admit Me?*
2. *What* can *I Contribute* to this Institution?
3. *What* makes *Me Unique?*
4. *What Distinguishes Me* from the other applicants?
5. *Why* MUST this Institution *Admit Me?*

The answers to these questions must be compelling, powerful, and #THOUGHTFUL.

When you have the requisite GPA and standardized test scores, Passion may just be the proverbial game changer in an application.

Everything is Relative – you think it is tough getting accepted to an Elite School? It is even more competitive getting that job offer. You must always showcase your intellect and prowess to prove how your skill set will be an #ASSET and #ENHANCE any environment.

In my estimation, #PASSION is the most important selling point of an Elite applicant. Passion is an intangible quality that can only be quantified through the student's 'life work.'

This is the 'What makes you tick' factor. It is also how you can distinguish yourself from everyone else.

OPTICS AND THE APPLICATION

OPTICS is simply the way the applicant is presented to admissions on paper. The goal is to make the optics as favorable as humanly possible. This enhances the chances of making it past each round of the application process. I am not saying that we are creating an optical illusion of the application, nor are we turning an unqualified applicant into a qualified compelling applicant.

Instead, my focus is on the *presentation* of the credentials the applicant already possesses to specifically *maximize* impact on the admission committee and the Dean.

CHAPTER 24

THE PAUSE BUTTON

Now hit the proverbial #PAUSE button...

STOP. BREATHE. THINK.

Time for #HOTYOGA or #PILATES or #SPINCLASS or just take a walk, a hike, or sweat with my Fitness Trainer Friend #TRACY.

The Elite School Admission process is overwhelming for everyone. It is especially important for parents to *step back* and *evaluate* how their kid is doing on an emotional and academic level. The reality is that, as parents, we must be *sensitive* to the needs of our child.

Speaking on behalf of myself, despite pushing my kids to get straight 'A's and to achieve in and outside of school, I have always maintained that their emotional well-being is of the utmost importance.

Your children, despite being smart, are teenagers with brains that are not fully developed until age 25. High school is never an easy playground for any teenager to navigate. These days it seems harder for our kids to attend high school because of social difficulties more than academic challenges.

As I previously discussed, the social pressures that our kids confront start in middle school, and do not get easier. For an adolescent, navigating the high school social landscape can be far more challenging than learning AP Calculus.

Why? These kids, and they are just kids, are bombarded daily with sensory overload from social media and electronics. Their brains are not fully formed to deal with every day social peer pressures that include introduction to a variety of drugs and alcohol. Oh yes, this happens in everyone's backyard. No one is immune.

Kids are taught to read and write but are not taught how to interact socially. I am aware that high schools are not etiquette schools, but to me, an observant parent, there seems to be tremendous social pressure placed on our teenagers, and they are not being given the resources and tools they need to *cope* with everyday life.

In fact, many kids between the ages of 14 and 28 suffer from depression and anxiety. It is not only astonishing but disturbing to me that so many kids are *suffering.*

Why is this and how is this being addressed? This chapter is titled "The Pause Button" for this reason. Everyone must stop for a moment. Parents must look at their kids and take the time to know how they are doing.

If your kid or someone else's kid is experiencing depression or similar diffi-culties, the first goal should *not* be to get into a top Schools. Rather, you should focus on the kid's #EMOTIONAL state of being. Remember that chap-ter on the #HAPPYFACTOR?

This book addresses a critical juncture where we prepare a high school se-nior's application for Schools. As a parent, you must understand all that is in-volved in this process.

The #REALITY is that up to this point in a high school senior's life, they may have been pushed so hard or worked so hard that they did not assess how they were feeling.

The #PAUSEBUTTON allows everyone to breathe and actually *pause* for a mo-ment. This is the time, in August, just weeks before senior year starts, when students should *reflect on what they have accomplished thus far, who they are as a person, and what they envision for their future.*

Kids also need to #REFLECT on their emotional and social wellbeing. Pro-spective Schools not only have to be a 'fit' an applicant on an academic level, but also on a social level. In many ways, the social aspect outweighs the aca-demics. The Number 1 ranked Elite College or University may not be the best fit for your kid. #REALITYCHECK.

August is the time to finalize the College wish list and determine the #REACH schools and the #SAFE schools, which are the 'within the realm of reasonable probability'. As we have discussed throughout this book, if your kid knowingly applies to Colleges where there are 'no chance in hell' of *ever* getting accepted, they have more or less given their informed consent for rejection.

Please try to dissuade your kid from sending applications to the 'no chance in hell' Colleges. The money will be better spent on a new pair of jeans or shoes! Again, this is just how I would prefer to spend my cash, on me for a change, rather than a tutor.

I decided to place this next piece in the "Pause Button" chapter because my friends will agree that many of their kids who are currently in their 20s, who did in fact graduate from top Colleges or Universities, are #DIRECTIONLESS. They do not have the tools to be successful in the 21st century. Was attending College worth it? What did they get out of that College?

At this juncture of the College application process as a parent or mentor, the priceless guidance that you provide is to look for a College and/or University that is a #TRUEFIT for the applicant.

Sometimes that Designer Label top just does not fit you well. It may look great on the rack, or even on someone else, but it just is not right for you. I know this is a silly way to draw a comparison to selecting a College, but it is true.

It sounds great if your kid wants to attend an Elite Schools, but it just might not fit them well.

#WISEWORDS: Your kid should PICK THE COLLEGE OR UNIVERSITY THAT IS THE RIGHT SCHOOL FOR THEM!

CHAPTER 25

STRATEGY TO APPLY:

Early Decision, Early Action, Regular Decision

T here are three ways in which an applicant can apply to College – Early Decision ("ED"), Early Action ("EA"), and Regular Decision.

Choosing which method to apply can be the difference between an acceptance and a rejection.

All Colleges and Universities accept applications via Regular Decision, although not all Schools utilize Early Decision or Early Action. Some Schools will offer applicants an ED 1, EA 1 and ED2 and EA 2. The dates are staggered for these two ED and EA filing options to give the applicants who were rejected from their first filing choice the opportunity to pick a second choice ED 2 or EA 2.

There are significant distinctions between the three application submissions. Most Schools provide a chart that delineates the specific application component requirements and deadlines as it pertains to each filing classification.

Most parents and, surprisingly, students do not understand what ED and EA means, nor do they have any clue as to why one would utilize either submission. ED typically has a universal deadline for filing of November 1st.

WHY ED IS IMPORTANT TO THE DEAN OF UNDERGRADUATE ADMISSIONS

In August of a student's senior year of high school the #FIRSTCHOICE Elite

School should be selected.

"Why?" you ask. Based on everything that we have discussed thus far, every applicant is a #LONGSHOT to be accepted to an Elite School. In my opinion, the high school senior ought to identify their 'first-choice' School no later than August. This comes down to #STRATEGY. Once that first-choice School is selected, the process to formulate a strategy to get accepted to that College or University begins. The clock starts ticking my fellow parents...

When your kid picks that first choice, then my next suggestion is that your kid apply to that College or University ED. I will write this in plain English so everyone reading this will understand the importance of ED. Since it is next to impossible to get accepted to any Elite School, the applicant *MUST APPLY ED!*

APPLYING ED SIGNALS THE DEAN THAT THE APPLICANT WANTS TO ATTEND THIS SCHOOL!

When an applicant applies ED, this is the #SIGNAL to admissions that the applicant really, really wants to attend this school in the fall.

This is the shout out to the Dean, 'Hey, look at me, your School is my #1 choice! I really, really want to attend!'

An applicant can only apply to 1 ED School. ED is a Binding Contract that the student (and parent!) signs. In the event the applicant is accepted, he/she is contractually obligated to attend the school and remit payment for the first year of tuition. This is serious and is not for the flaky, indecisive student. If the student does get accepted ED and breaks the contract by attending another school, they can be exposed to financial liability in the amount of the first-year tuition payment.

My fellow parents, YOU are on the HOOK for that cash!

Yes, applying ED is important in securing an acceptance early. ED notifications are revealed around mid-December. What an incredible #RELIEF it is if your kid does get accepted ED. You are all done with applying to Schools. #BESTGIFTEVER!

Then you have the *other* kid. The other kid who 'can't make up their mind' as to which school they want to apply. Better yet is the kid who 'wants to apply regular decision because they want to see *which* Elite Schools will accept them'. #LOL.

Like most kids have that #LUXURY, where they can submit applications to Elite Schools and then mull through all the eventual acceptances. Duh, No.

Most kids are not in the position to be accepted to several Elite Schools and have the power to choose which one they will attend. #FORGETIT!

Early Action is another smart choice for applying to Schools. Some Schools offer EA 1 or EA 2. #EA is not binding, which is a great relief to all jittery, indecisive students. You get to play it safe. In this scenario, your kid can pick a school they really want to attend, that may be a bit of a reach, apply early, and learn whether they are accepted or rejected early. This is still better odds for getting accepted EA, because this is not the regular decision pool.

The Regular Decision applicant pool is where everyone throws their hat in the ring, and this is where all the application submissions jump exponentially. As we have discussed, this is when the chance for acceptance is lower.

CHAPTER 26

ANXIOUSLY WAITING...

Waiting, waiting, waiting. #SUCKS. As a parent, it is my hope that you mentored your child to the best of your ability, and that your kid is still standing after this entire process. Moreover, that your relationship is still intact, and peace is restored in the family home.

The waiting period starts when the applications are submitted and the official deadline for all applications to be filed passed. This is a remarkably interesting time, like being in the eye of a hurricane. #SERIOUSLY.

All I can say that you must wait. The work has been done.

CHAPTER 27

CONCLUSION! HALLELUJAH!

Ah my dear, fellow Parents. We are at the end of the road of our journey. It is my hope that the #WISEWORDS I have imparted upon you all, will provide some guidance as you embark on your Schools journey as a parent.

As parents, we all walk down similar paths, and wanted to share some of the #FUNFACTS I accumulated throughout my own College journey with my sons and their friends.

My prayer is that the College or University your child ultimately attends will serve as the foundation for your he or she to #FLOURISH on an emotional and intellectual level. It should be a place where they are able to be with like-minded peers and incrementally mature as an adult. As a parent, you want your child to study in an environment where they can pursue their passions and attend an institution that will provide multiple platforms for them to accomplish their goals.

REMEMBER: Parents – we already attended College! The College our kids' will attend does not validate us or our performance as parents.

FYI: *Do not take it personal* if or when your kid gets #REJECTED from one or all the Elite Schools they apply to. Conversely, the same type of logic rings true to our kids if *they* are confronted with rejection.

We have briefly discussed the importance of emotional happiness, and how this happy factor can influence current and future academic performance. We all acknowledge that high school can be difficult for our teens on an emotional and social level. Sometimes, our high achieving, intelligent, socially awkward high school KIDS, seek the *affirmation* of their intellectual and academic abilities through an acceptance to an Elite School. In fact, for some kids, the acceptance to an Elite School is the *social validation* of their peers that they ultimately seek.

Thus, it is of the utmost importance to ensure that your student is a Qualified applicant and meets the Elite School's Rubric requirements. The completed application must be the embodiment of all that the student has accomplished not only academically but reveal an engaged, creative, self-motivated thinker and leader. Once that is completed, the student can know there is nothing else to be done.

Regardless of which College or University accepts your kid, it is my hope that they have a positive self-esteem, positive self-image, are happy and should be proud of their accomplishments thus far. These Institutions do not define us; to the contrary, we define and enhance them based on our unique attributes and individualism.

I enjoyed sharing my #WISEWORDS. Thank you for coming along on this journey!

#GOODLUCK #PEACEOUT

ACKNOWLEDGEMENT

My sons and husband made this book possible. Parenting is not easy, by any stretch of the imagination. Our shared goals for our kids to be extraordinary, showered with excessive amounts of unconditional love, mutual admiration, thoughtfulness, kindness and perseverance made their successes possible.

As for my boys, they humored me, and chose to be #EXTRAORDINARY...

THE ADMISSIONS GAME   Get Your Kid Accepted To
College and Do Not Go to Jail!
Published by Amazon Kindle Direct Publishing
ISBN-13: 978-1070642635
ISBN-10: 1070642630

acceptedschools@gmail.com

Made in the
USA
Lexington, KY

55948810R00090